THE MINICOMPUTER SIMPLIFIED

THE MINICOMPUTER SIMPLIFIED

An Executive's Guide to the Basics

Carol W. Brown

FP

THE FREE PRESS

A Division of Macmillan Publishing Co., Inc.

NEW YORK

Collier Macmillan Publishers

LONDON

THE FREE PRESS
A Division of Macmillan Publishing Co., Inc.
866 Third Avenue, New York, N. Y. 10022

Collier Macmillan Canada, Ltd.

Library of Congress Catalog Card Number: 80–1031

Printed in the United States of America

printing number

1 2 3 4 5 6 7 8 9 10

Library of Congress Cataloging in Publication Data

Brown, Carol W.
The minicomputer simplified.

Bibliography: p.
Includes index.
1. Minicomputers. I. Title.
QA76.5.B776 001.64′04 80–1031
ISBN 0–02–905130–4

Contents

Preface

You must have said to yourself, "Is it time to consider getting a small computer for my business?" as you heard how popular they were getting and how prices are dropping. Maybe one or more of your friends have taken the plunge. Maybe a hungry salesperson has already found you and painted a picture that sounds too good to be true. Maybe a competitor has boasted of his tremendous satisfaction with his new system and how his business has improved. Maybe another friend suffered endlessly in getting his system going and told you a real horror story.

You want to look into the facts and make your own decision but have been put off and have felt ill at ease with the lingo and the novel concepts and the high-pressure salesperson and the strange-looking machines. You continue to postpone the investigation, hoping that at some point either computers will get easier or you will get smarter about them!

This book is intended to make you smarter about computers. It's been written by a person who's been through all of it, with lots of hands-on experience in the many aspects of matching minicomputer solutions with business needs. The information in this book will help you make educated decisions about the place for a minicomputer in your business.

I am grateful to a lot of people. Special thanks go to attorney Bob Blumberg for help with Chapter 14, on contracts. Thanks also to Gail Pyle for providing me with a friendly electric typewriter, the correction key of which I have worn to a nub. Bob Wallace at The Free Press provided encouragement when my confidence ebbed and was wonderfully patient and considerate. My husband, Cyrus, always believed I could do it and made it all possible in a myriad of ways.

THE MINICOMPUTER SIMPLIFIED

CHAPTER ONE

Enough Computer Jargon to Get By

The purpose of this chapter is to give you enough computer vocabulary to get by. The terms I discuss will get you through a sales presentation without looking or feeling ignorant.

It is unfortunate for everyone involved that computers always seem to be discussed in a foreign language. It immediately puts the uninitiated at a disadvantage. Knowledgeable computer people use jargon as a shorthand way of communicating with each other. But even they have trouble keeping up with the acronyms and terms that are constantly being invented and bandied about.

Computer jargon comes in several varieties. First, we have acronyms, which are seemingly meaningless words made up of the first letters of meaningful words. Some acronyms are pronounced as words, such as ROM (pronounced "rahm"), which stands for "read-only memory," a term you can immediately forget. Other acronyms have their letters pronounced separately, as in CRT (pronounced "see-are-tee"), which stands for "cathode ray tube." (Cathode ray tube is a fancy name for something that you could consider a black-and-white TV set with a typewriter keyboard built into the bottom of it.)

Our friends at International Business Machines (you undoubtedly know that acronym) are inveterate users of acronyms. When the IBM salesperson comes to call, ask him to avoid using acronyms. The length of his visit may double, but you will save yourself a lot of confusion.

Another kind of computer jargon is the so-called weird word.

The one that most often strikes terror into the heart of the non-user is "byte" (pronounced "bite"). If you substitute the word "character" evey time you hear "byte" you will have no problem, as a byte is just that, a character. The word "byte" has four bytes in it. The name "Carol Brown" has eleven bytes, as the spaces between words of text are often counted as bytes, too.

Normally bytes are discussed when people are talking about how much storage space a computer system has. A computer that can store a million bytes is smaller than one that can store 5 million bytes. By the way, the nickname for one million bytes is "megabyte," which is abbreviated MB. When a salesperson says that a computer has 50MB, he means that the computer has the ability to store 50 million letters and numbers simultaneously.

Another kind of jargon is the one-letter word. The letter K is used a lot in computer talk. It means a thousand characters, the same kind of characters we talked about as being bytes. Thus, 64K means 64,000 characters. Usually, when salespeople talk about how many K a computer has, they are describing the size of its "central processing unit," also called CPU or "memory." The more K a computer has, the more versatile it is likely to be. Later we will discuss what happens inside the CPU.

A lot of other jargon consists of strange words used for perfectly normal things. Take, for example, the term "input-output device." This term is fancy language for a machine that can both *give* and *receive* information. Your mouth could be considered an input-output device, as it both accepts food and drink and produces speech for others to receive. Your ears and eyes, however, would normally be considered "input-only" devices. Other parts of the body would be considered "output-only" devices. The printer on a computer system is logically considered an output-only device, as it can only produce information and is unable to receive information from the user. A terminal with a keyboard attached to it can display information to an operator and accept information through its keys; thus, it qualifies as an input-output device. The acronym for input-output is I/O (pronounced "eye-oh"). Frequently you will hear the term "I/O devices" used to describe the entire group of input-only, output-only, and input-output devices that surround and serve the central processing unit by giving information to it from the user and returning information from it to the user.

Some words that are very familiar to us are used in specific ways in computer talk. These words represent concepts that are important to understand. Several of these terms are interrelated, and you'll need to feel comfortable when they are used by others.

Let's say that you had a list of customers with whom you had done business over the years. Computer people would refer to this list as the customer "file," meaning a collection of related information. In this case, each name shares with each other name the relationship of being your customer. Each customer name would occupy one customer "record." In other words, each customer would constitute a *record* in the customer *file*. A customer's record contains all the pertinent information about the customer, including perhaps name, address—street, city, state, zip code—and current balance. Each of these facts would be considered a "field." A field is a discrete fact, or piece of information, within a particular record. And each field is made up of bytes. Isn't it a little bit like "the frog on the bump on the branch on the log . . . "?

Files, records, fields, and bytes will come up as computer salespeople attempt to "size your files." In simpler words, they want to figure out how large a computer they can justify selling you. They will attempt to identify your major files, estimate the number of records in each, determine the likely fields and their size within each record, and eventually come up with the total number of bytes of storage required for the jobs you need done by the computer.

Let's use another example so that you can prove to yourself that you are comfortable with the terms "file," "record," and "field." An inventory *file* would normally contain information about all of the products a company carries. An inventory *record* within the inventory *file* would contain a lot of facts about one particular product. One of the *fields* within an inventory record might be the selling price of the product; another *field* might be its name.

Computer people often want to describe a field by its format or appearance, as well as by its contents. They may use the words "numeric" and "alphabetic" to do so. When they say a field is numeric, they mean that the field should contain only numerals, say, a dollar amount or a domestic zip code (many foreign zip codes use letters). Fields that have only letters in them are called alphabetic. Many fields have a hybrid format, containing both letters and numbers. Accordingly, they are called "alphanumeric" (or "alphameric" for short). An example of an alphanumeric field is a street address, which typically includes a house number and a street name.

Why do computer people care whether a field has numbers, letters, or both? Well, there are some considerations involving the way numbers and letters are stored in a computer, but the best reason for caring is yet another acronym, GIGO (pronounced "guy-go"), which stands for "garbage in, garbage out." This is a frequently heard—and apt—phrase.

Once bad information gets into a computer system, it will almost certainly come out the other end, perhaps many times. It is in everyone's best interest to prevent bad data from getting in. And one of the ways to validate the information put into a computer is to test its format. As a down-to-earth example, if an operator is requested to enter a dollar amount but accidentally hits a letter instead of a number, the system should reject the entry and ask for re-entry. We will discuss this topic in much greater depth later on.

We have been discussing data here. "Data" is a term you will hear often in computer talk. You might hear, for example, "Programs and data are stored on the disk." Just what is "data" and how is it different from "programs"?

The data in a system consists of all the information about the customers, products, receivables, orders, payroll, and every other area the system processes. It is the *data* that is being *processed* for the user. The data in a system is the most valuable part of the system to the user. Visit a fire drill in a midtown Manhattan office building sometime and watch the people carrying disk packs containing all their data files out to the street! The physical machinery can be replaced easily; obtaining complete, up-to-date lists of your customers, products, and orders would take much more time and effort.

"Programs" are the instructions the machines follow to process a user's data. There are several varieties of program, which we shall discuss in greater detail subsequently. But keep in mind that without some sort of program in it, a computer is utterly and completely *stupid*. It is dumb to the point that it cannot add or subtract or print or display anything on a screen. It does not know the date or the time of day and can't do anything the least bit useful without a program!

This brings us to the terms "hardware" and "software," which no salesperson will ever fail to use. Hardware refers to all the machinery that is involved with the computer. Hardware can be touched and seen and heard and watched. Some people even call it "iron." Software, on the other hand, is the general name for all of the programs that make the system operate. You cannot see software in action, as it is, in its simplest form, merely electricity coursing around inside printed circuit boards within the central processing unit. Because of its amorphousness, its intangibility, people call it software.

In general, there are two kinds of software, and it is helpful to be aware of the difference between them. "System software" comes with the machine, from the manufacturer, and is the general name for the set of programs that make the machine know *how to run itself*. Another name you will hear for this is the "operating system." Each manufacturer's operating system is different because the hardware being operated is itself different. Manufacturers like to boast about their operating systems and their ingenuity. True, the job of the operating system is to run the machine itself as efficiently and reliably as possible. Like a traffic cop, the operating system decides which user shall have control over which device. For example, if two users each ask for a printed report, it would not make sense for the computer to combine the reports into one! The operating system must grant to one user the use of the printer until his report is printed and place the other user in line to wait briefly. So the operating system has to be a fairly smart program, well designed and well written, as it becomes the boss of the entire system. Indeed, the quality of the operating system has a great influence over the way a given machine performs. Remember that the operating system is software but usually comes along with the hardware from the manufacturer.

The other kind of software is "applications software." This is the general name for all of the programs that perform the specific jobs to be done in your business. Examples of applications software are programs that perform order entry, accounts receivable, general ledger, and accounts payable functions.

If all businesses performed their functions the same way, the job of installing computer systems would be infinitely easier! Obviously, this is not the case. Businesses operate in unique and diverse ways. Therefore, the computer programs they need to assist them may be very different from one company to the next, even when the companies are direct competitors. Applications software is generally unique at least to the industry involved, if not to the company. Remember, applications software is the group of programs that perform your business applications, no matter where the programs come from.

The concept of a language is not strange to most of us. Even if we haven't actually traveled abroad, we understand that if we go to a foreign country, we might either speak that country's language or go without communicating verbally, as the people there will not necessarily understand our language. The same is true with computers. Computers have a language of their own, which we do not understand easily. In general, the language a computer understands is called its "native language" or "machine language." Each machine has its own machine language. Were we to see machine language, it might be all ones and zeros or strings of meaningless letters and numbers. With some effort and quite a bit of knowledge, we could decode the machine language, but it is very difficult and wasteful of time and effort to try. The machine doesn't understand our language either, although over the years we have come closer and closer to that idyllic state. Programming languages have been developed so that people can give instructions to computers in people-language (or as close as possible to people-language). Once people give their instructions, a translation process takes place. A special program called a "compiler" tries to translate the people-language into machine language. As with any language, in order to be understood, one must follow rules of logic, grammar, and syntax. Computer languages have their own vocabularies and rules of grammar, logic, and syntax. If the writer has obeyed the rules, the compiler will be able to make a successful translation of the instructions into machine language. Interestingly enough, the compiler itself is also a program, whose job it is to turn the user's program instructions into something the machine can understand. The concept of a special language for a computer is not difficult. Think of a translator at the United Nations translating a speech for the delegate from the country called Computerland. Each salesperson you see will tell you what language his computer uses and boast of its wonders. We will continue the discussion of the various computer languages in Chapter 4.

With the advent of minicomputers, people have begun to give more consideration to the nature of "interactive systems." What is an interactive system?

In the early days, computers were so expensive that you couldn't have one in the middle of your office. The computer was located in a central location so that all the users (who were helping pay its enormous bill) would visit it, bringing their own work to be done. Such systems operated in what we call the "batch mode." They would do your job for a while, then mine, then someone else's. While your job was running, mine was not. In fact, my data existed in the machine only when my job was actually running. When my job was over, I would take my data away, and you would put your data in the machine and run your batch of work. Each of us would have up-to-date totals right after running our jobs, but not again *until the next time* we ran a job; so we got our information from our batch system at intervals. Generally, system designers tried to set the size of that time interval to be consistent with the costs and benefits inherent in producing the information. For example, if you were producing quarterly financial statements, it was fine to accumulate information for three months and then visit the computer. But can you imagine running an airline reservation system that way? The businesses that really had to have information *quickly* (it's called "real-time" when it's almost instantaneous) began to spend money on developing interactive systems. These systems gave their users almost immediate responses to requests and transactions. If a ticket agent reserved a seat on a given flight, the very next agent to query that flight would be shown one less available seat. You can see how different this sort of processing is from batch processing. It's an important distinction to remember, as now real-time, or interactive, processing is available to minicomputer users and may be something you will want to consider carefully.

This next section will be fun to read since it is going to cover phrases you don't need to bother with! Human minds are sometimes perverse, however, and you will probably remember the meanings of these terms because you don't have to.

A "bit" usually gets mentioned along with the ubiquitous byte. Bit is a shortened form of "binary digit." Suffice it to say that there are eight bits in a byte; their coded makeup tells the computer what character the byte is. You should not have to worry about bits. But, after all, the computer has to know one byte from another somehow, doesn't it?

Another weird word that sounds like something from the Wild West is "baud," often used in the phrase "baud rate." Baud means "bits per second" and refers to the speed at which devices can exchange information over communications lines. The whole subject can be dropped until your computer system grows to the point where you want several locations talking to each other.

A few other terms worth ignoring are "microsecond," "millisecond," and "nanosecond." They are all names for unbelievably small fractions of seconds within which computers can perform discrete operations. Salespeople will try to impress you with how fast the computer can go. You are much better off asking down-to-earth questions like "How many invoices can I print in an hour?" or "How long will I wait for a response to my inquiry to the system?" Frankly, you really shouldn't care whether the inside of the computer is full of hamsters on treadmills or mirrors or gnomes so long as it does *what you need done.*

A final word on the subject of jargon. You wouldn't be totally wrong if you had the suspicion that computer jargon is a conspiracy to make computers sound more difficult than they really are. Some of the world's biggest braggarts are people who have the least to claim for themselves. In the same way, some of the people who use the most computer jargon really know the least about computers. Don't be afraid to ask for plain English from salespeople, consultants, programmers, or anyone else who starts to spout computer talk. And add a little extra skepticism to your judgment about anyone who tries to wow you with a lot of jargon. They wouldn't do it if they really cared whether you understood what they were saying.

CHAPTER TWO

Just What Is a Minicomputer?

Within our short lifetimes, computers have been invented, refined, and dramatically improved.

Few of us were able to view the ENIAC, developed in 1946 at the University of Pennsylvania School of Engineering. That computer was used for calculating ballistic trajectories. The ENIAC filled several rooms with its eighteen thousand vacuum tubes. In addition to the electrical and reliability problems caused by the sheer number of tubes, the amount of heat generated, which had somehow to be dissipated, was enormous. The ENIAC became the UNIVAC, also enormous, inefficient, and unbelievably expensive.

In those early days, only big, well-funded research sites and big, well-financed companies (and of course the government) could afford computers. They were placed in specially air-conditioned rooms with special electricity and strengthened floors raised to allow hundreds of snakelike cables to run beneath. White-coated technicians hovered around the equipment much like worker bees attending their queen. Some technicians actually were located within the computer itself! Programmers agonized over tortuous programs written in machine language that were impossible to create and even worse to test and correct. Somehow the rest of the world got the idea that these machines possessed extrahuman intelligence, calling them "giant brains" and worse. Books like Orwell's *1984* further encouraged the fear of computers and their Big Brother potential.

Computers did get cheaper, smaller, and easier to operate in the fifties and early sixties. Most large companies and some medium-sized ones obtained their own computers. This class of computer received the name "mainframe computer" or simply "mainframe," as they usually constituted the company's centralized data processing facility.

Most data was prepared away from the computer, in the form of punched cards. Operating departments of the company would submit large batches of paperwork to employees called "keypunch operators," who would "type" the relevant data onto punched cards. Those cards would then be processed by the computer in large batches. The resulting reports would be returned to the operating department sometime later.

The machines themselves performed one job at a time. The vacuum tubes were gone, replaced by transistors. The mainframes were still tended by technicians, now without white coats. The equipment still lived in heavily air-conditioned rooms with raised floors but was easier to program and operate. Memories were larger, and communication with the user improved. Programmers of this era were drawn to their vocations by a love of machinery and problem-solving and were not known for their normal or socialized behavior. In fact, at one point long hair, a beard, sandals, and an Indian belt around the forehead seemed to be the programmer's uniform!

The term "minicomputer" is extremely difficult to define in specific terms. The term used to mean small. In the early days of computers it meant home-built, such as a bright engineer might construct in his basement in his spare time, or special-purpose, such as used in specialized industrial applications. Indeed, the early minicomputers were developed for very specialized industrial and factory tasks, for example, controlling an oven or keeping a chemical solution at a constant acidity. Since the early computers themselves were so large, these special-purpose computers seemed small in comparison and thus received the "mini" designation.

The dividing line between a minicomputer and a mainframe computer has itself been getting fuzzier over the years as both have become substantially larger. Today's minicomputers are frequently larger than yesterday's mainframes! Suffice it to say that defining a computer as a minicomputer based upon its memory or disk storage capability has turned out to be a short-lived solution. Similarly, calling computers below a certain price minicomputers fails as a workable definition because the prices of the components of computer systems have fallen dramatically since the early days. To illustrate this point, IBM has estimated that calculations costing $1.26 to perform in 1952 can now be done for seven-tenths of a penny!

For a time, the definition of minicomputer had an unspoken element of "not from IBM," in addition to the "smaller than a mainframe" aspect. This was because IBM really did not enter the interactive minicomputer marketplace until the late seventies. For a good ten years, the other manufacturers had the minicomputer marketplace to themselves. Now that IBM, too, has strong offerings in this field, the entire minicomputer movement has increased credibility and would appear to be strongly entrenched in the computer scene.

Perhaps the only definition that will stand the test of time is that a minicomputer is a computer system that does not require a raised floor! Today's minicomputer normally does not need the extensive and expensive air-conditioning and electrical arrangements of the mainframes of the past. Often they do not require their own computer room but are located in the departments they serve. They are designed to co-exist well with the people who use them and function at the same temperature and humidity as their users! They are substantially smaller than the early mainframes, as the vacuum tubes were replaced by transistors, which in turn gave way to semiconductors. Indeed, now "microcomputers" physically smaller than minicomputers are common; their entire processing logic and internal memory are contained in a single "chip" smaller than your fingernail. Entire computer systems no larger than a desk or a desk top are common.

The people who operate today's minicomputers are no longer professional keypunch operators but normally are ordinary office staff members, perhaps the very people who performed the same applications manually before the minicomputer system appeared. Most often data is not keypunched into cards but is entered directly into the system via a terminal, or CRT. Normally the work is not batched but is entered as it occurs or is received, at which time the system's files are immediately updated, as in real-time processing. The systems are commonly able to run more than one job at a time, and the jobs are designed to have interactive dialogue with the user. This means that the operator's entries are requested one at a time in simple English terms and are tested for validity. Should the entry be invalid for some reason, the operator is informed of that fact, again in simple English terms, and asked to reenter the data. In this way, the operator can be led through rather complicated entry sequences and can correct errors on the spot.

In many ways, today's minicomputers should be considered office tools like copiers and typewriters. The term "small business computer" probably makes more sense in defining the function of today's minicomputer in the business environment.

Moving the computer out of the computer room and onto the user's desk has had some dramatic effects on the organization and management of many companies. When computers were terribly expensive and difficult to operate, there was no choice but to centralize the data processing function within the business in order to operate efficiently. One of the results of extensive centralization was the creation of computer "empires" within companies. The user departments whose data was being processed had to submit their work to the centralized facility and wait to get it back. Conflicts frequently arose in part because many users were not good at communicating their needs and desires to the computer facility. On the one hand, they were unfamiliar with data processing concepts and practices; on the other hand, the computer department was not brimming over with patience and spoke that dreadful computer jargon. The managers of computer facilities often judged their own success by the amounts of new and sophisticated equipment they could amass for their operations. Top management, wringing their hands over ever increasing expenditures that they could neither understand nor prevent, exacerbated the trouble by failing to set computer processing priorities. In some companies where the costs of the central computer facility were "rebilled," or charged against the user departments, warfare broke out. Small wonder, then, that minicomputers that could belong to single departments and be under local control have become very popular indeed.

Large companies that have decentralized their computing resources have been able to delegate to their managers clearly defined areas of responsibility and accountability. And they have been able to analyze profits and losses in these areas once they were not dependent upon a central computing facility.

We can see that the minicomputer has really taken the opposite role from that of the giant, decentralized mainframe.

Whatever its storage capability or the number of users attached to it, a minicomputer is a "nearby" computer, dwelling alongside its users and helping them in their everyday work.

Never in the history of computing has there been such a variety of computing devices available to businesspeople at so low a price. Accordingly, the small businessperson and the department manager in a bigger company are the target of intense marketing efforts.

In the next chapter we will discuss the various devices that make up a minicomputer.

CHAPTER THREE

What Does a Minicomputer Look Like?

There are presently numerous kinds of minicomputer. There will be many more to come. Inside racing cars specialized minicomputers monitor gasoline use. There are minicomputers inside toys that teach children to spell and to identify words. Small calculators are approaching the level of minicomputer and can amortize your bond or calculate your biorhythms while being held in your hand. There are minicomputers in Las Vegas alongside traditional one-armed bandits. One model accepts your money, displays pictures of spinning fruits and bells, and flashes "WIN!!!" on the screen in vibrant colors if you hit the jackpot; if you lose, it displays encouraging and consoling messages and exhorts you to play again.

Within all this confusion, there exists a class of computers referred to as "small business computers." Although they are made by various manufacturers and are used for diverse tasks, they have much in common. It is this class upon which we shall concentrate.

The Small Business Computer

Small business computers perform the same basic functions regardless of physical differences among them. First, they *take* data from the user, possibly testing the data and preparing it for storage. They then *file* data for subsequent retrieval. Data need not necessarily be filed in the same sequence in which it was taken.

They *move* data around from one place to another within the computer, possibly sorting, collating, merging, or purging it in the process. They *process* data by performing arithmetic and logical operations on it. Finally, they *print* data, usually in the form of reports.

In order to help you appreciate the differences between one small business computer and another, let us review each of the devices that might possibly form part of a minicomputer system.

The Central Processing Unit

As I have said before, the central processing unit, or CPU, acts as the brain of the entire system and contains its memory. The term "memory" differs from the term "storage" in that memory is used to hold the job instructions and data actively being processed, whereas storage contains jobs and data not being processed at the moment.

If you were to look at a central processing unit, you would see a metal box, or chassis, perhaps the size of a grocery carton. Often there is a strange array of lights blinking furiously on the front, giving the impression that there is tremendous activity going on inside. These lights, more than any other single aspect of a computer, tend to intimidate the uninitiated. The non-user usually assumes that everyone else but he understands the cryptic meaning of these lights. The opposite is true! Most programmers find no meaning in the lights—they are useful only when they stop flickering and then only to diagnostic or service personnel. Don't let the lights make you feel ignorant!

It is always a shock to look inside the central processing unit and see nothing moving! Perhaps you will notice a fan rotating in order to dissipate heat. Otherwise looking inside a computer is pretty boring.

The chassis has slots along its edges, into which printed circuit boards are inserted. They may stand on end perpendicular to the floor or they may be stacked horizontally. Either way, there is a surprising amount of air and open space inside the CPU, and there are hardly any moving parts.

Printed circuit boards are the heart of the computer. On them are mounted the transistors, capacitors, chips, and other electrical marvels that create a computer. Their undersides have ribbons of solder, through which electricity flows. It is not necessary for you to have the foggiest idea how all this works. But do consider how small, lightweight, and portable the printed circuit boards are. Each board has a special function: some provide memory for the computer; others provide the processing and arithmetic logic functions; still others convert the power supply to and from the required voltages.

When your system breaks down, which fortunately happens much less frequently than in the past, the serviceperson can bring a replacement printed circuit board, or even several boards, in an average-size briefcase! He will replace any board not functioning correctly with a good one and take the bad one back to his service location to be repaired. In the meantime, your system is up and running! This "modular replacement" arrangement is a decided improvement in computer technology: previously, servicepeople did lengthy diagnostic and repair activities at your location while you waited to regain use of the machine.

Should you care what is going on inside those circuit boards? Some salespeople will tell you about the "cycle times" of their systems, trying to impress you with how fast the system can do a thousand simultaneous additions without interruption. This may indeed sound impressive, but it is not likely that you will ever want or need to do a thousand back-to-back additions without such interruptions as gathering more data or printing a total. Even if you deliberately chose a system with the fastest available internal speeds, there is no guarantee that your applications will be executed more quickly. Many other factors affect the speed at which a system runs: the quality of the programming, the structure of the files, and the design of the system all enter into the determination of the final result and operating speeds. If you are considering a very unusual machine for a highly esoteric application, pay careful attention to the machine's internal operating speeds. Otherwise, assuming you are reviewing competitive machines from the major manufacturers in the minicomputer marketplace, you would be wise to ignore differences in internal speeds until all other factors appeared to be equal.

Memory Size

You should be very interested in the amount of memory contained in the central processor. Remember K, the term for a thousand characters of memory? Generally, the higher the K, the more expensive a processor is. Also, the greater the K, the more jobs that can likely be run at the same time and, to some extent, the faster each job will run. To make a very rough analogy, consider trying to rearrange the items in your desk. First, try this without any work surface to place the items on in the process. Then imagine how much easier the job becomes if the entire top surface of your desk is available. A computer goes through a similar reshuffling process during most jobs and often can operate much more efficiently when given a little breathing space.

By and large it is fairly simple to add more memory to a computer by inserting another printed circuit board—if you have been careful to choose a system that permits expansion. In plain terms, there must be another slot available in the chassis. It is difficult to predict exactly the right amount of memory needed to run a system ideally. Before the programs are written and the files converted, estimates will be made that inevitably prove low later. It is important to be able to add memory if early estimates were off, if new applications are added, or if the company's growth outstrips early projections.

On some systems, the amount of memory required to operate effectively is directly related to the number of devices (usually terminals or printers or other equipment involved in exchanging data between user and computer) attached to the system. In other words, each device gets its own permanently allocated portion of the computer's memory for itself. This portion is often called a "partition" of memory, and we call this fixed method of allocating available memory "partitioning."

In nonpartitioned systems, all available memory is made available to all active users at the time, usually on a demand basis. The more users simultaneously handled by the system, the less relative attention each gets.

With partitioned systems, the user who wishes to add another device (usually an entry terminal) can get a nasty shock when he discovers that he may have to add more memory to do so or worse that he has no room for more memory. On the other hand, the addition of another device to a partitioned system will not slow down any of the other users, as each user has a separate memory area permanently allocated to him.

In a nonpartitioned system, the more the system is burdened with additional devices, the more reshuffling it has to do and the more slowly it will operate.

The term "response time" is used to describe the ability of a system to respond to users' commands. It means the amount of time that elapses between a request for attention from the system (usually accomplished by hitting a key labeled "Enter" on a terminal) and the satisfaction of that request for attention. Up to five seconds can be tolerated, depending upon the nature of the application. Response times of ten seconds or more are very difficult to tolerate in an atmosphere of high interaction with the terminal, as the "cadence" of effective entry will be destroyed by continual waiting.

Be sure to find out from your salesperson whether the system he wants to sell you allocates memory among its devices by partitioning. If it does, find out whether the addition of more devices requires the addition of memory. Find out how much each increment of memory costs and whether there is a limit on how many increments can be added. Initiate a discussion about response time with your salesperson at the same time. Be specific in questioning the effect that additional devices may have upon the promised response time of the system.

"What Are Those Things That Look Like TV Sets?"

Terminals that resemble TV screens with typewriter keyboards in front are common devices on minicomputers. They go by many names, the most common being CRT, an acronym for "cathode ray tube," the principal internal component of such terminals. Other names are VDT, an acronym for "video display terminal," "screen," or just plain "tube." No matter what you call such terminals, they have revolutionized data entry methods for business computers.

The term "keypunching" refers to the primary method traditionally used to prepare data for mainframe computers. Keypunching requires specially trained operators who enter data into cardboard cards, using special machines that punch rectangular holes. The process is clumsy and cumbersome in that if a wrong hole is punched, the entire card of eighty characters has to be replaced. Indeed, the keypunch machine is a rather ungiving device, providing the operator with relatively little feedback about whether the data being keypunched is correct, except for a crude test involving numeric and alphabetic characters. In addition, the operator does not, and cannot be expected to, understand the content or purpose of the data being prepared.

Many errors can be introduced into data during the keypunch process. In the effort to reduce their incidence, more specially trained keyboarders operate machines called "key verifiers" and rekey the data keypunched earlier. This time, the machine compares the data being keyed to the holes on the card that was previously punched. The verifier can thus identify some of the errors the keypuncher has made. Of course, this step delays the entry of data into the system and causes double keying expense.

Even a two-step keying procedure cannot detect errors caused by illegible or incorrect source documents. Normally the first step in preparing data for a mainframe computer is to edit the data. Generally this means passing the data through a program that takes totals of all numeric fields and looks up all coded fields in master files and tables. The program also performs various kinds of logical checks, depending upon the nature of the data. This "edit program" then prints out a list of the errors it has found. The listing may be sent back to still another group of people, the "control group," who look up the source documents and resolve the errors as best they can. The offending punched cards are then corrected, reverified, and the data is finally pronounced to be "clean" enough for actual processing.

If you found the above explanation a bit tedious, the actual process is also tedious. In general, the preparation of data for computer processing on mainframe computers takes the data away from the people who have originated it and places it in the hands of others, who add their own errors. The computer then identifies some, but not all, of the errors. The data is given to people who can resolve the errors, corrections are made, and processing takes place. The process is clumsy and rife with delays and expense. The results, in terms of error-free data, are not good. All of us have had the experience of trying to communicate with a recalcitrant computer, say, at a department store. Much of the trouble could no doubt be traced back to difficulties encountered in getting the right data into the machine in the first place!

Happily, entering data into a minicomputer system through a CRT terminal can be relatively easy. First, the operator can see exactly what is being keyed on the screen. The keypunch machine makes this impossible to do. Should a mistake be noticed, usually only the offending character need be rekeyed, not the whole transaction. Better yet, through thoughtful programming, the operator may be provided with a form on the screen that very much resembles the source document being entered. A flashing character called a "cursor" can be positioned at the location where the operator is to fill in the blanks on the form, guiding the operator through the required entries. Prompting text can be used to make requests of the operator, such as "Enter telephone number, area code first." Should the operator enter something that the program has been designed to reject, a straightforward message about the nature of the error may be displayed, such as "Zip code must be numeric. Please rekey." As the operator is keying, the program controlling the operation can be testing all entries in every possible way, through inquiries into tables (for example, "Is MX a valid state?") and/or logic tests ("Is the middle digit of the area code a zero or a one?").

You should now have a sense of the huge difference that this style of data entry can make. We call this style of processing "interactive," as there is constant interaction between the operator and the computer. With interactive data entry through CRT devices, even the novice operator can follow the step-by-step requests being made by the system. And if the system is well designed, the quality of the data being entered in a one-step (no verifying!) operation can be much higher. Think seriously about including interactive data entry in your plans for a computer system. And pay particular attention to the CRT devices offered by manufacturers.

What Should a CRT Be Able to Do?

The size of the screen is a prime consideration. Screens range from one-line displays on some hand-held terminals to full size—1,920 characters, which is 80 characters across and 24 lines deep. Unless there is some overriding reason to do otherwise, it would be wise to consider a full-sized screen for most applications. The full-sized screen allows for the display of a generous amount of data and permits maximum flexibility in the design of an interactive procedure, allowing the operator to inspect large amounts of data and instructions at one time and leaving ample room for prompts and error messages.

Several other screen features are useful and effective in designing a strong interactive system. One is "dual intensity," a method whereby some characters are displayed more brightly than others, under the control of the program displaying the characters. In simple terms, this allows some data to be highlighted. A popular use of dual intensity is to have the prompting text (the words "name," "address," "city," "state," "zip," etc.) *less* intense, or "in the background," and the data keyed by the operator *more* intense, or highlighted. The highlighted fields are sometimes said to be "in the foreground."

Another useful feature is called "reverse image." Normally on a screen, either dark letters are displayed against a light background or light letters are displayed against a dark background. One terminal permits the user to have either arrangement, depending upon the setting of a switch in the back of the terminal. At any rate, through reverse imaging the normal display mode can be reversed for individual fields on the screen, again under the control of the program displaying the data. This facility is useful for highlighting significant fields that must have the immediate attention of the operator, perhaps such as serious errors.

"Audible tones" such as beeps and clicks are also useful features. A beep may be sounded by a program to signify an error or the need for additional data. The click feature assists the operator in establishing a keying cadence, as the sound can be emitted each time a key is depressed.

There are still more useful features available. Some terminals have the ability to blink and/or to underscore certain data, again varying the appearance of important data and highlighting it for the operator.

All of the features mentioned so far can help the operator if they are used in a consistent, well-conceived, productive way. The various keys on the keyboard must also be considered in terms of the operator. The presence of large numbers of strangely marked keys, over and above what most people are used to on a typewriter, can arouse great apprehension in a novice operator. From a training point of view, it is ideal to be able to greet a new operator or user by saying, "Sit down at the keyboard. It looks just like a typewriter keyboard. The machine will give you instructions all along the way and will not let you do anything wrong." Some terminals have numerous extra keys that have to be learned and understood. If you are reviewing terminals and notice unfamiliar keys, be sure to ask their functions and to determine whether the benefits to be gained by them outweigh the confusion they will inevitably cause.

What to Look for in a Printer

Computer printers come in a number of shapes and sizes. The one thing that they have in common is that they all use paper in continuous form that has pin-feed holes along each edge. The pin-feed holes fit on sprockets within the printer that carry the paper through the printer in a continuous flow. The paper may be single part (one-ply, no carbon) or have up to six leaves, perhaps separated by layers of carbon paper. Duplication is accomplished either by interspersing carbon layers between the parts or by using specially treated paper ("No Carbon Required" is one variety) that creates a copy upon impact. The paper may be plain (called "stock" by most users), covered with the familiar green-and-white bands, or preprinted with logotypes, headings, and columns appropriate to the user's application. Preprinted checks with register stubs are a common type of preprinted form and are used for accounts payable. In this instance, the bank MICR numbers are also preprinted.

Basic Kinds of Printer

Computer printers come in several varieties. One variety prints one letter after another across the printed line. Another prints the whole line at one time.

The first variety is called a "serial" or "character" printer. It functions very much like a typewriter, printing one letter after another across the page from left to right. A few serial printers take advantage of the return trip that the printing element has to make to come back to the left margin, and they also print from right to left on the return trip, effectively doubling the printing speed. Serial printers may actually be modified typewriters, often of the kind with the "golf ball" printing element. Other serial printers use different means of creating a fully formed character, such as a "daisy wheel" printing element. A "dot-matrix" printer creates each character by printing the appropriate dots in a very small (one character size), five-by-seven dot rectangle. Dot-matrix printers can print Chinese characters as easily as the ones you are now reading, as the configuration of the dots for each character is under the control of the computer and not the printer. People find dot-matrix printers attractive more because of their low price than because of their ability to convert to Chinese or Japanese characters easily, however.

Often serial printers are used as terminals and have keyboards built into them. In this way, the entries of the operator and the responses of the computer may be retained in hard copy form. The trade-off for this documentation is the fact that the fill-in-the-blanks approach previously described becomes less feasible because of the time required to print the entire form on paper. Very few printers are able to reverse the direction of the paper so that the operator could begin entering data at the top of the page after the bottom of the form had been printed, as would logically occur on a CRT terminal. Obviously, the decision to use a printer terminal in lieu of a CRT terminal would depend upon the particular application.

"Line printers" are much more sophisticated and generally more expensive devices. As their name implies, they print an entire line at one time. This is accomplished by a moving chain or drum, which has a number of sets of the alphabet whirling at high speed. When the appropriate letter is opposite the proper print position, a hammer pushes the paper against the chain or drum for the briefest fraction of a second. When you consider that there are usually only five of the letter A on a print chain and that these printers can print entire lines of 132 A's at the rate of several hundred lines per minute, you have to appreciate the split-second timing mechanisms engineered into a line printer. And, as you might suspect, with so many moving parts working so quickly, printers tend to break down and malfunction more often than the other solid state devices on a computer. We will talk further about the kind of systems design and programming that can minimize the effects of the problems that occur when the printer breaks. Even so, consider the printer to be a device with very delicate innards, upon which you will be fairly dependent.

There is a third variety of printer, the "electrostatic printer." This kind of printer creates the electrical image of the entire printed page and then prints it all at once on specially treated paper. It can make only one copy but it can do so at very fast speeds. Electrostatic printers are relatively expensive, and it is unlikely that you will be invited to consider one in your search for the ordinary small business computer.

What Difference Does Printed Page Width Make?

One of the aspects of computer processing that usually comes as a shock to the first-time user is the limitation of the width of a computer printout. Most computer printers have a maximum of 132 print hammers. Some have fewer, say, 120 or 80. With 132 hammers, only 132 characters, including blanks, can be printed across a given line. Of course, an infinite amount can be printed line after line, or until the paper runs out. But there is a fixed, almost universal limitation of 132 printed characters horizontally. Most printers print ten characters to the inch, which converts to a printed line 13.2 inches wide. What does this mean to you? It means that the reports and forms your computer system produces will have to be designed with this limitation in mind. You may not be able to fit all twelve months of sales for this year and twelve more for last year on the same printed line. Most people learn to live with this limitation fairly easily. It is only mentioned here so that you will not have unrealistic expectations and a nasty shock!

What Other Limitations Are There?

As long as we are on the subject of things the printer can't do, here are a few more. The printer can't roll the paper backward to add something to a line already printed. It (usually) can't print some things in a different color, say, red numbers for credits. It rarely can turn the letters sideways, as would be the case when labeling the vertical axis on a graph. And don't disappoint yourself by planning to print more than six copies or parts. In fact, the sixth part (fifth copy) can be pretty illegible on the best of printers; it depends upon the quality and thickness of paper and carbon and how well the printer has been adjusted. It is asking for trouble to design a system that requires successful six-part printing!

Storing Your Data

Disk Storage

Most business computer systems employ some sort of disk storage device. As I said earlier, storage devices hold the instructions and data that are not currently being used.

There are several kinds of storage device. The most popular are "disk" (also spelled "disc") and "magnetic tape." We will talk later about magnetic tape. Here, however, it is useful to review the major difference between disk and tape.

A reel of magnetic tape is very similar to the tape you might play on your tape recorder at home. If you wanted to play a selection recorded in the middle of your reel of tape, you would have to advance the intervening tape past the playing heads in order to reach the part you wanted. The same is true on a computer. For the computer to read the data in the middle of a reel of tape, it has to advance the intervening tape past the tape heads. For this reason, people call magnetic tape a "sequential access" device; that is, the data has to be accessed in the sequence in which it was recorded.

Disks work differently. The recording surfaces, usually one or more platters that resemble long-playing records, spin at high speeds around a central spindle. The read-write heads dart back and forth above, below, and between the surfaces, approaching and retreating from the central spindle. With the surfaces revolving and the heads moving across them at high speed, data anywhere on the disks can be accessed in roughly the same amount of time on average. There is no requirement to access data from the beginning of the disk to the end, for there is really no beginning and no end! Because the computer may go directly to a given data location on a disk, disks are called "direct access" or "random access" devices.

What Does Disk Storage Look Like?

Disk storage is made up of two separate assemblies. First, the "disk drive" contains the motors and timing mechanisms to spin the recording surfaces and to move the heads. Second, the disk itself (sometimes called a "disk pack") is inserted within the disk drive to be spun, read, and written upon. Some types of disk storage do not permit the disk to be removed from the disk drive by the user. Others allow removal, and users remove one disk and insert another very much the way you change records on a turntable. A hybrid arrangement contains two disks, one removable and one fixed. Both disks are driven by the same motors and read by the same arm of read-write heads, thereby cutting manufacturing costs somewhat while providing the convenience of removable disks.

Is it Good to Be Able to Remove Your Disks?

Yes, it is. The disk storage devices will usually contain all of your files of customers, orders, inventory, and other important information. Copies of your programs will be stored there, too. You will want to take frequent copies of all the contents of your disks for security reasons. Being able to remove the physical disk packs from the drives allows you to make these copies quickly, assuming you have at least two disk drives. We will speak more of file backup later, but while you are reviewing manufacturers' offerings of disks, think about the subject. Make sure it will be possible, and relatively simple, to make copies of your data and programs.

Disks and drives come in all shapes and sizes. The smallest are called "diskettes" or "floppy disks" as their recording surface is made of a relatively flexible material. They resemble 45 rpm records and come in a protective paper envelope. Twenty or thirty of them could easily be transported in an average briefcase. Correspondingly, they do not hold a great deal of data compared with larger disks. Diskettes may vary somewhat from system to system but usually hold between 250,000 and 500,000 characters each. Frequently the diskette drive is contained within the cabinet of the central processor or some other device, as it is not too large. There may be multiple diskette drives, allowing two, four, or more diskettes to operate simultaneously. Each drive can be identified by a slot into which the diskette is inserted, usually covered by a little door.

"Cartridge disks" are large and normally round; they have the diameter of a good-sized pizza. The recording surface looks like a 33 rpm record and is covered by a case of durable plastic, from which it should not be removed by the user. The disk is loaded into its drive with a flat, sliding motion, again very much the way a pizza is put into an oven. Cartridge disks are often of the hybrid variety mentioned earlier. The cartridge forms the removable part, and beneath it is a permanently fixed recording surface without a cover, under the control of the same motors and read-write heads. Cartridge disk packs are not as easy to transport as diskettes. A strong man could carry eight of them in two specially built satchels. Each disk weighs three to five pounds and contains room for 5 to 10 million characters, depending upon the manufacturer.

Even bigger disks have drives that from the outside resemble top-loading washing machines. The disk packs themselves have multiple recording surfaces stacked like platters, with spaces in between. The entire arrangement is covered with a clear plastic cover when out of the drive. Thanks to the platter-stacking arrangement, these disks hold a great deal of information, perhaps up to 100 million characters of information, again depending upon the manufacturer.

During the late 1970s, we saw an incredible increase in the number of characters that could be stored on minicomputer disks and a corresponding decrease in the prices of such large-scale storage devices. While the 1980s may not witness such dramatic changes, be sensitive to the trends when reviewing disk hardware for your small business computer. A little careful shopping may pay off with big benefits!

Magnetic Tape

Yes, disks do sound wonderful. But does it mean that magnetic tape is on the way out?

Mainframe systems are heavily dependent upon magnetic tape as an input-output medium. The early systems used such tape almost exclusively. The typical system had numerous tape drives, and many were used for each job; a typical job involved reading in one tape with input data on it, processing the data in the computer, and writing out another tape with updated output data on it. Frequently data was sorted by packaged sort programs. Often a whole row of six or eight tape drives would be kept busy reading and writing the intermediate results of the tape sorting process.

Along the way, magnetic tape became standardized so that tapes written by one machine could be read by another machine, perhaps from a different manufacturer (although one manufacturer never joined the movement toward compatibility). Even today, magnetic tape is a medium frequently used to exchange data between computers that may be very different in other ways, as there is an industry standard format for its use. For example, many corporations report their data to the Internal Revenue Service on magnetic tape. You might easily purchase a mailing list or other useful data on magnetic tape.

Magnetic tape is cheap and easy to store. There are countless instances in the operation of a minicomputer system when you might want to retain data for future use but not want to devote active, day-to-day storage space to keep the data in your computer system. Writing the data off onto a reel of magnetic tape, which costs less than $20, is a cost-effective solution. At some time in the future, you could read the data back into the computer from the magnetic tape and perform any desired analysis or processing.

People with systems whose disks are not removable must use magnetic tape to copy their data for back-up purposes. A special utility program is used to copy all of the programs and files onto tape. The tape is then retained for security purposes and, if needed, can be used to reestablish data lost in the system.

As you can see, the need for tape has not disappeared with the advent of minicomputers and their enlarged capacity for cost-effective disk storage. Standardization of disk formats for minicomputers is a long way in the future. It is now, and will continue to be for some time, impossible to use a minicomputer disk in any other computer except its twin! For compatibility reasons alone, magnetic tape remains a most useful device to have in any computer system.

How Does Magnetic Tape Work?

Anyone who has worked with a tape recorder will have no difficulty understanding the workings of magnetic tapes in computers. Both systems record by magnetizing a pattern of particles of ferrous oxide affixed to a tape base. Both have a reel-to-reel winding mechanism that advances the tape at a specified rate and allows the functions of rewinding, stopping, and starting to be performed. Both allow the tape to be used and re-used many times and erase recordings by recording over previous contents.

Computer magnetic tape may be read or written upon numerous times. In order to prevent accidental erasures, all systems, by industry standard, require that you insert a plastic ring into the hub of the tape reel in order for writing to be performed on the tape. The phrase "no ring, no write" is universally quoted to help the user remember when the ring is required.

How Does One Tape Differ from Another?

You will hear the words "channel" and "track" mentioned: they mean the same thing. Early magnetic tape drives utilized a coding scheme in which every character was represented by a unique combination of seven magnetizable spots, aligned in a column. The spots were either "on" or "off" (magnetized or not) depending upon the pattern for the character being written on the tape. The arrangement of the spots in rows of seven led to these early drives being called seven-track or seven-channel tape drives. More modern tape drives use a slightly different coding scheme that involves nine tracks or channels. Although seven-channel tape drives are still in use, it is getting more difficult to find them. It would be preferable to have a nine-channel tape drive today in order to have the maximum compatibility and convenience.

You will also hear the word "density" used. This refers to the distance between the columns of spots. Early tape drives wrote their characters at a density of 556 bpi (bits per inch). Technology has made it easier to put more data into less space, so now you will commonly see tape drives that write at densities of 800, 1,600, or even more bits per inch. Drives with densities of 800 and 1,600 are common in the industry today. In fact, many drives have the capability of both densities, depending upon the setting of a switch. Either affords accuracy and convenience. Of course, 1,600 bits per inch will use less physical tape than 800 to write the same amount of data. This aspect can be important to a user if a given amount of data really needs to fit upon one reel of tape. An example of this might be a job performed when the computer is unattended, that is, when there might not be anyone available to mount a new reel of tape on the tape drive when the first reel became full.

Finally, there is the speed at which the drive advances the tape for reading or writing. This is expressed in inches per second (ips). The tape drives that are normally available with minicomputers are, as a class, slower than ones available for most mainframe computers. This means that it may take longer to read or write the same tape on a minicomputer than it might take on a mainframe computer. When shopping for tape drives, try to find the fastest one possible that is consistent with the price and use you plan for it. In other words, if you plan to use the tape drive only occasionally, high speed may not be worth the extra cost.

Punched Cards

You will not frequently find a small business minicomputer using punched card readers or punches. This is because of changes in the methods of data entry that we discussed previously. The few manufacturers offering these devices on minicomputers do so only to allow them to be compatible with older systems that employ punched card devices.

You may have information on punched cards you would like to put into your new computer system. Consequently, should you consider buying a punched card reader? Probably not. As a one-time conversion step, the punched cards that you have can be taken to a service bureau and converted to magnetic tape, diskette, or perhaps disk. It may be somewhat cumbersome to arrange the conversion, but in the long run it is worthwhile to advance to a system that allows the kind of interactive data entry discussed earlier.

Paper Tape

Paper tape, like magnetic tape, is a sequential access device. However, recording is accomplished by punching holes in paper. Time-sharing computer users frequently use paper tape to prepare their data in advance. The paper tape is inserted into the teletype to be read into the mainframe computer at top speed. Paper tape is slow to process as it moves at a fraction of the speed of magnetic tape. It is also difficult to store and should be avoided in your small business computer system unless there is a compelling reason to use it. Many systems do not include paper tape devices in their range of available peripherals.

Communications

Communications is perhaps the most confusing area of peripheral devices for computers. Certainly it is the most technical area and uses the most jargon!

There are several reasons why you might find communications devices useful adjuncts to your small business computer system. The first reason could occur even before your system was totally finished. If your source for programming has access to your system through communications, and you have a problem during the shakedown period, the difficulty can be resolved over the telephone; the programming vendor can quickly correct the problem from a remote location, saving you a great deal of time. Many users find a communications linkage to their programming resource to be very helpful in resolving the inevitable problems that are part of the growing pains of a new system.

The more traditional use for communications is to link remote users to each other and to a central computer. The remote users may actually be computers themselves. The linkages may be through ordinary telephone lines or through specially conditioned leased lines, perhaps using private communications networks. Rather complicated arrangements can be made in which computers poll each other on a prearranged schedule. Many messages per second are transmitted and received in such systems.

Obviously you will not start your system at this level of communications complexity. On the other hand, you could very well develop this sort of requirement and you want to be able to accommodate it.

Having a remote terminal using communications facilities to contact your computer is easy with most systems. You will have to obtain the necessary communications hardware, normally an additional printed circuit board, from your hardware vendor, as well as a special device called a "modem." Modem stands for "*mo*dulate-*dem*odulate," the functions performed on the signal that is communicated and received. Modems come in all shapes, sizes, and prices, depending upon the speed at which communications take place and various other features. One feature, "automatic answer," makes the computer able to answer its own telephone when it receives a call. More expensive modems with fancy features are called "data sets"; they are available from the telephone company and other sources. Less expensive modems, called "acoustic couplers," generally have rubber gaskets into which a phone receiver fits. Acoustic couplers may be found separately or may be built into small, portable printers or terminals.

Once you have your communications hardware and your modem or data set, you may receive calls from anyone else who has a modem and an input-output device. The calling party could be your software vendor, a remote branch office of your company, or your company president calling from home. The caller would be treated like a local terminal. Naturally, you would want to take some precautions that not just anyone could call your computer. This can be done easily, even with automatic answer, by limiting both the distribution of the computer's telephone number and the times of day when automatic answering is available.

If your communications needs appear to exceed this level of complication, you are best advised to seek professional communications advice at the time of hardware selection.

Optical Readers and Mark Sensors

These specialized input devices read either special type fonts or mark-sensed cards. A few minicomputer manufacturers include them in their line of peripheral devices—at fairly high prices. If you are a first-time computer user, you would be wise to go the conventional terminal data entry route at first, adding these devices later if the volume of data entry transactions and your particular application demanded it. You may well find that the advantages you gain from interactive data entry make it unnecessary to use scanning or sensing equipment to enter data. Including such requirements in your search at the onset may unnecessarily limit your hardware choice.

CHAPTER FOUR

What Makes the Computer Go?

People who are uncomfortable about computers often feel that way because they know they cannot answer the question "What makes the computer go?" They may ascribe superhuman intelligence to computers in trying to explain how they work. This notion must reflect the publicity computers received in their early days, when they were described as giant brains able to know all, see all, and do all. Some recent horror films have reinforced this misconception by starring monster computers that talk, walk, and run amok, threatening their owners and the entire world! No small wonder, then, that many people feel uneasy around computers.

If computers were supposed to be omniscient, so were the people who tended and worked with them. Accordingly, along with the giant brain, came the mad computer scientist complete with white lab coat. He alone could control his creation, but some of this aura settled on everyone able to communicate with computers.

Let's get rid of these notions right away! *Computers are really stupid!* And the people who operate them are just like anybody else.

How Can Computers Be Stupid and Do All Those Wonderful Things?

Well, first, they are very good at *remembering* long lists of duties, even for years at a time. The duties will be *done exactly the same way* every time. Its jobs may be very repetitious, but the computer will do them *countless times* without becoming bored or rebellious. And the computer can perform most tasks *much more quickly* than a person can.

However, *a computer can do only what it has been told by people.* It has no ability to decide what should be done or to modify its behavior to suit a change in its environment without having been told how to do so in advance.

What Is a Computer Program?

A computer program is the way people tell computers what to do. A program is *a collection of instructions that together perform a particular function.*

For example, there is no doubt a program at the motor vehicle department in your state that prints your driver's license after you send in your renewal payment. There is a program at your bank that prints your monthly statement. And give this a thought: there is a program at the Internal Revenue Service that reviews your tax return and decides whether it will be tagged for an audit.

In Chapter 5, we will review the process of writing a program and discuss how a good program differs from a bad one. In this chapter, we will review all the different kinds of programs that work together in a system to make the computer go.

The Operating System

The computer is *so* stupid that it cannot even advance the paper in the line printer without the guidance of a program. There is an important program that helps the computer operate all the physical devices attached to it. More accurately, a group of programs performs this function: it is called the "operating system," the "executive," the "supervisor," the "monitor," and many other names and/or acronyms that usually imply *control.*

The operating system, which actually *controls the machine*, normally comes with the hardware from the manufacturer. In general the operating system differs from one machine to the next and is thus considered unique to the machine it operates. Acting as "command central," the operating system decides what resources of the system can be employed by various users at various times.

Here are several examples of tasks that an operating system might perform:

—display a question on the terminal, as requested by *another* program, such as "Do you have more entries? Enter yes or no."

—receive the response from the operator of the terminal, either "Yes" or "No," and pass it along to the program that made the request

—locate and run the particular program requested by a user

—send a printed line to the line printer, print it, advance the paper one line, and notify the program producing the report that it is ready to print another line

—act as a traffic cop so that when two users want the same device at the same time, only one is allowed to proceed; the other is made to wait (for example, two terminal users might want to print a report on the line printer at the same time; a report combining and interspersing each one's data would look foolish indeed!)

You might be surprised by some of these examples and have said to yourself, "I would have thought the programmer would have had to take care of all those tasks." And you are right. At one time the applications programmer did have to write programs that physically managed all the devices on the system. Today's modern operating systems have taken much of this burden from the applications programmer, allowing him to concentrate on the user's requirements for the applications involved.

The operating system is a complex group of programs usually written by a special team of programmers, called "systems programmers," at the manufacturer's. Much attention goes into the construction of the operating system so that it will run the machine as efficiently as possible. The everyday computer user is generally not able, and certainly not well advised, to modify the operating system.

What Does the Operating System Mean to the User?

As a user, you should be aware that the operating system is an important component of your computer system. It has substantial influence over the operations of your computer system.

The operating system can place restrictions upon the expansion capability of a system, restrictions that are not necessarily imposed by the hardware devices themselves. For example, the operating system may allow only eight terminals to be attached simultaneously even though more than eight are physically possible. Likewise, the operating system may direct data to the line printer at much less than its rated print speed, reducing printing speed substantially. In short, the operating system has an effect on *every device and function*.

How Can an Operating System Be Evaluated?

Operating systems vary greatly among manufacturers. The ideal operating system would do four things simultaneously:

1. Operate all functions and devices at maximum speed.
2. Take up minimal storage and memory space.
3. Assume many burdens that would otherwise be borne by the user's programs, such as exchanging data between devices and handling conflicts between users.
4. Be versatile, flexible, bug-free, easy to change, easy to understand, and easy to shift from one system to another.

As you might expect, some operating systems do some of these things. None does all, as these tasks themselves are mutually exclusive! An unfortunate few do none of them very well.

It is terribly difficult, if not impossible, to judge an operating system by itself. Imagine judging a traffic cop without any traffic! Ideally, one could take the same user program, operate it on different equipment with different operating systems, and compare the execution speeds and the space required to operate the program on each machine. This technique, called "benchmarking," is a traditional method of comparing mainframe systems.

Benchmarking becomes a less useful tool when attempting to compare minicomputer systems. Because minicomputer languages vary widely from one manufacturer to the next, the program to be benchmarked may not run on all the systems being compared. Alternate versions of the program may have to be written and run. Comparison of the systems is then muddied by differences that may have been introduced by the change in language and the rewriting of the program. Another reason why benchmarking is more difficult with minicomputer systems is that these systems are often designed to run *interactively*, that is, with frequent dialogue and interchange of information between system and operator. Any tests of speed and performance must take the operator's speed and performance into account. Otherwise, programs chosen for testing must be limited to those that run without operator intervention.

We will speak again about operating systems. The main ideas to remember about them are:

—Operating systems are special, complicated groups of programs that handle the computer's operations and make applications programming easier.
—They come with the machine and are different for each computer.
—They substantially affect machine performance.
—They cannot be judged alone.

Applications Programs

You have probably been asking, "But where are the programs that do *my* jobs?" Your computer system may be printing customer statements or calculating trajectories of rockets to the moon, but the overall name for the programs that do *your* jobs is "applications programs."

The computer system exists for the purpose of running applications programs. The operating system should make these programs easier to design and run them efficiently. The hardware devices have been chosen for their ability to play a particular role in the application, such as print checks, store transactions, or read magnetic tapes.

There is no hard-and-fast rule about what goes into an applications program. Normally there is some purpose to be accomplished or function to be performed by such a program. The important idea here is that the particular function or purpose of one applications program may be a very small one. Most jobs are actually performed by large groups of small programs rather than by one giant program.

As an example, an application that is frequently computerized is "accounts payable." It is very unlikely that the accounts payable application would ever consist of just one program, for there are many individual functions to be performed in order to operate the complete accounts payable application:

—set up a permanent vendor record
—enter a vendor's invoice
—list all open items present, sorted by vendor
—select open items for payment, perhaps by due date or by vendor or individually
—print vendor checks on check stock after aligning checks in printer
—print the check register
—post the general ledger
—run the month-end trial balance as an audit trail
—run a listing of cash required at certain dates
—purge the resolved items from the system

It would be impossible to write one program to do all the things listed above. First, the program would be so enormous that it could run only on the most gigantic central processors, if at all. Second, it would be nearly impossible to test and debug because of its size. Third, it would be dreadfully inefficient, as the instructions to perform all these functions would have to be loaded into the computer at one time, while logically only one or two of the functions would ever be carried out at the same time! Thus, it makes much more sense to have each function programmed as a separate module. In this way the modules would be of a workable size, and each one would be loaded into the system only when its function was to be performed. During the rest of the time the module would be stored.

Where Do Applications Programs Come From?

Applications programs are written by "applications programmers," a label used to differentiate them from systems programmers, who write operating systems for manufacturers, as we have seen.

There are about as many varieties of applications programmer as there are applications! Common sense dictates that the applications programmer not only know how to program the computer but be competent in the area of the application as well. Imagine an accounts payable applications programmer trying to program rocket trajectories to the moon, or vice versa! This simple truth seems to have escaped a great many people over the years, and a lot of computer horror stories have had their origin in the fact that the programmers responsible did not understand the application to be programmed.

Two Different Approaches to Applications Programs

The user who wishes to obtain a computer system generally has two choices. He can choose to have a "custom system," which is specifically written for his particular use, or he can look for a "packaged system," in which case he looks for programs that have already been created and adjusts his procedures to conform with the existing programs. The obvious analogy here is that of buying a custom-made suit from a tailor as opposed to buying a ready-to-wear suit off the rack. If your measurements are somewhat unusual, you may be unable to fit yourself into the ready-to-wear suit and opt for the generally costlier custom suit. Likewise, custom systems will almost always cost more than packaged systems but may be worth the higher price.

Some applications are amenable to packaging. For example, two companies in totally different businesses may operate their accounts payable in a fairly similar fashion. The same can be said for the general ledger functions and (although less so) accounts receivable. Applications that tend to differ greatly from one company to the next are those that are most closely involved with the actual products or services being sold, such as order taking, inventory control, sales history, and customer history. These applications tend to vary with the line of business the company is in, the products or services it provides, its marketing philosophy, and a myriad of other factors that make companies unique.

Even in the areas that do lend themselves to packaging, there are numerous differences in the ways in which companies wish to perform their applications. In Chapter 10 we shall discuss each of these applications in turn, reviewing the features that well-written, comprehensive packages should include. At this point it is important to note that there are strong packages and weak packages, cheap packages and expensive packages, and that the word "package" does not necessarily mean panacea.

How to Choose between Package and Custom Programs

Fortunately, like the ready-made suit, package software can be inspected before you buy it. If the decision to shop for custom software is not a clear-cut one, it is often helpful to investigate and to see various packaged systems in action. Usually a good demonstration of a package enables the potential user to visualize how his applications would (or would not) work using the package. If numerous demonstrations of packaged software fail to convince you that one would fit the bill, chances are that custom software should be sought.

Are Application Programs Different on Minicomputers?

Yes, they can be quite different from their counterparts run on mainframe computers.

We have discussed the interactive environment several times before. The *opportunity to operate interactively* on minicomputers causes almost all applications to be run differently on minicomputers from the way they have been on batch and mainframe computers in the past.

Again, using accounts payable as an example, a minicomputer programmed to operate interactively can perform a number of desirable tasks that would not be possible using older, batch-style programs on mainframe computers.

Example One

> The operator neglects to specify the vendor for an invoice. On a batch system, the omission would be identified on an "edit program," which might be run hours, if not days, later. A printout specifying the omission would be returned to the appropriate department asking for completion of data. On a minicomputer system, the program would perhaps display a message such as "Vendor code is required" on the operator's terminal and refuse to proceed until a valid vendor code had been provided. The problem would be resolved within seconds, or minutes at the most, and involve only the operator.

Example Two

The operator provides a valid vendor code for the transaction but the code has been assigned to "Acme Mechanical" rather than to the correct vendor, "Acme Machine." Depending upon the quality of the edit procedure, the batch system might catch this type of an error, resulting again in the printed incorrect message's being returned to the originating department hours or days later for correction. If the error were not detected, the system would produce a check for the wrong vendor, whose records will certainly be confused by the unsolicited payment. Confusion will result and at best time and effort will be required to retrieve the erroneous payment.

The minicomputer system can minimize the chance that the operator will use a valid but wrong vendor code; it does so by displaying the name and address of the vendor whose code has been entered and asking for confirmation from the operator that this is the desired vendor. Having entered the vendor code, the operator receives a display like this:

```
VENDOR CODE          :   123
VENDOR NAME          :   ACME MECHANICAL CORP.
VENDOR ADDRESS       :   123 MAIN STREET
                         ANYTOWN
                         NEW YORK
                         12345

IS THIS THE VENDOR YOU WANT ?  (Y/N)   :
```

The operator now compares this name and address with the invoice billhead. Seeing that the invoice says "Acme Machine," the operator types "N" in answer to the question on the screen and proceeds to obtain the right code. Manual procedures may dictate that the operator lay the miscoded invoice aside for someone else to obtain the correct code, or the code may be obtained on the spot. The important aspect of this example is that the erroneous code *did not enter the computer.*

Example Three

An accounts payable invoice transaction normally includes posting(s) to the general ledger. These postings explain the nature of the expense, such as telephone, rent, repair, raw materials, or other expenditures. Basic rules of accounting demand that these postings, when totaled, equal the amount of the invoice, so that all debits equal all credits and the books are in balance. In a batch system, should the operator make a keyboard error that causes the postings not to equal the

> amount of the invoice, the edit program should catch the error later and the (now familiar?) printed error notification would be returned to the originating department for correction. In a minicomputer system, the program controlling the operator's entries would immediately point out that the debits and credits to the general ledger were not in balance and prevent the operator from completing the transaction until correction had been made. Assuming that the operator's source document were correct, and that the error had been one of operator carelessness, the error would be corrected immediately. Otherwise the transaction may be laid aside for researching by others.

In general, most applications can be programmed interactively on minicomputers to operate *better* than their previous versions on mainframe computers. The computer, with *less trained personnel* can operate *more quickly* and with *more accurate data,* than before.

Improvements in the operation of many applications are not totally free. Along with the benefits, a new group of operational considerations has arisen. Since most interactive systems utilize multiple terminals, from which many users can operate the system, these considerations involve the way in which the system will handle several users wanting to do the same thing at once. Several aspects must be considered.

First, the system must have certain security features built into it since its users may be relatively untrained personnel who are not on the computer staff. Some personnel may be permitted to modify the data in the system, while others are allowed to inquire about the data but not to change it. Second, a subtle set of problems occurs when a second user wishes to display or modify data that is in the process of being changed by the first user.

We will discuss the programming ramifications of these considerations in more depth in Chapter 5. For the moment, it is important to realize that interactive minicomputer systems have the potential of greatly improving the operations of many applications.

What Is a Computer Language?

No doubt you have studied a foreign language at some point. And you know that each language has its own vocabulary, grammar, and syntax. Well, computer languages are no different, except that they are usually written but not spoken!

Computer languages were developed to help people communicate more easily with computers. In particular, they were developed to make it easier to write computer programs. In the early days of computers, all programs had to be written in the machines' own native language, which was basically all ones and zeros. Writing in machine language was tremendously difficult. It could take all day to write a simple program to add two numbers together. Changing the program afterward usually meant almost a complete rewrite. The trade-off between effort and results was so poor that certainly, if easier ways of programming had not been developed, computers would not have progressed very far by now.

Every machine has its own native, or machine, language that its circuits have been engineered to recognize. This language, if printed out on paper, would perhaps be all ones and zeros or might involve letters and more numbers. No matter what characters it included, you would not be able to read it, so cryptic and nonsensical would it appear.

A "programming language" is much easier to read and write. The programmer creates his program in the programming language, which is far simpler to work with, and his efforts are translated, or converted, into the native language of the machine involved. *The purpose of computer programming languages is to make programming easier.*

Vocabulary

Some computer languages have words in their vocabulary that intentionally have the same meaning to you and me as they do to the computer. Take, for example, the word "if." The language called COBOL has the phrase structure "If . . . . [something is so] . . . then . . . [do something] . . . else . . . [do something different]." Not too scary? Similarly, the phrase "go to . . . [another place in the program]" exists in several computer languages. This is not to say that you could pick up the listing of any program in any computer language and read it like a mystery story. You might recognize familiar words but still find the whole thing puzzling. But if you were to spend a little time learning the unfamiliar words, most of the confusion would disappear. Like most foreign languages, computer languages are surrounded by what we could call a "language barrier." Once most of the terms are understood, the whole thing seems a lot less difficult.

Grammar and Syntax

Remember my saying that what the programmer writes is translated into machine language? Such translation would not be possible if the programmer didn't follow the language's syntax and grammar. An example of a syntax requirement is that the word "if" must be followed by the word "then" in some computer languages. Another grammatical requirement is that the word "move" be followed by both an object and a destination in some languages, as in "Move name to invoice-address."

Each computer language has its own vocabulary, grammar, and syntax. The manufacturers publish reference manuals so that programmers will know the rules to follow for the particular language that operates on a machine. If you were to look at one of these books, you would probably be reassured and begin to feel that computer languages are not as scary as you once thought.

Does It Really Matter Which Language My System Is Written In?

Yes, in the long run, it could make a tremendous difference. Here's why. The unfortunate fact is that *someday a stranger will be trying to understand your programs.* By the term "stranger" I mean a person who had no part in creating your system and has no understanding of its functions. Whether you plan to obtain your programs from a software house, large or small, or as a package, or you plan to hire an employee in-house, this *will* happen at some point. Personnel turnover in the computer industry is extremely high (some estimate it at 30 percent) and show no sign of decreasing. You cannot count on having the creators of your system available to help you for the life of the system.

Having acknowledged this fact, how can you minimize its effects on you? By choosing your computer language carefully.

Make it easier to find help with your system throughout its useful life by picking a language that lots of people know well. It can be very difficult indeed to locate help if your system is written in "Crypto-Delight" or some equally esoteric language.

Use a language that facilitates documentation. Some languages are much more easily read than others because they use familiar words like "multiply," "perform," and "if . . . then." COBOL, for instance, might easily have this sentence in a payroll program: "Multiply hours times rate giving gross." The words "hours," "rate," and "gross" are defined by the programmer. The words "multiply," "times," and "giving" are defined by the language itself and have specific meanings. The meaning of the instruction is clear to any reader. Please notice, however, that the clarity of the instruction exists because of the programmer's choice of the words "hours," "rate," and "gross." The instruction could just as easily have been "multiply cow times pig giving horse," assuming the proper data had been set up in each of the terms, and the program would have executed just as well. But notice how much less clear the program would have been! Some languages are touted as "self-documenting" because of their ability to accept meaningful names for data elements and program functions. Do remember, however, that good documentation is a process that takes place only with the cooperation of the programmer. In summary, then, pick a language that makes documentation easier and then see to it that the necessary effort is made! This effort will pay off when the stranger has to acclimate himself to your system. A well-written, well-documented system is easiest to maintain.

What Are the Languages to Choose From?

New computer languages seem to emerge all the time. Others are popular only briefly. Here I will mention a few of the most widely used languages so they will not seem unfamiliar when you hear them mentioned.

COBOL stands for "common business oriented language" and has been highly popular for mainframe systems. Almost all mainframe manufacturers have provided the ability to run COBOL programs on their hardware. In recent years, with minicomputers becoming larger, cheaper, and faster, COBOL has made inroads into the minicomputer world, where central processors originally were too small and slow to run it. COBOL's good features are that it is relatively straightforward to write; it allows the programmer to give meaningful data names and labels and thus add clarity to program listings (if he wants to); and a great deal of government and industry effort has gone into creating *standards* for its functions, vocabulary, and syntax. When such standards are created, a language begins to be transferable from one kind of hardware to another. COBOL's bad points are that compared to other languages it usually runs rather inefficiently on most machines and it is terribly wordy and fussy to write. Leaving out a period at the end of a sentence can have disastrous results!

Occasionally you will hear someone talking about the "Cobalt" language. They are really talking about COBOL, and they obviously don't know the first thing about it.

FORTRAN stands for "formula translation." As COBOL was developed for business use, FORTRAN was developed for scientific and engineering use. In general, the language was intended to enable engineers and scientists to translate algebraic and mathematical formulas for computer use. FORTRAN was developed to work efficiently with numbers carried to a great many decimal places or using exponential expressions, as in physics or in astronomical calculations. The language has been brought over into the commercial world to some extent and augmented with features enabling the programmer to carry figures to only *two* decimal places to express dollars and cents properly! FORTRAN programmers are not as easily located as COBOL programmers, but the language is considered a common one all the same. FORTRAN's assets are the ease with which it will allow complex calculations and the presence of industry standards for its functions. Its liabilities are the clumsy way in which it may handle simple calculations and manipulate commercial data and the possible difficulty in finding programmers with business experience.

BASIC began as a stripped-down version of FORTRAN developed for the time-sharing user. BASIC—"beginners' all-purpose symbolic instruction code"—is simpler and clearer than FORTRAN but still allows scientific expression. Recently it has gained widespread acceptance among commercial minicomputer users and appears to be emerging as *the* minicomputer language. Improvements in BASIC have made it possible to use meaningful data names, improving documentation and program legibility. Attention is beginning to focus on the development of industry standards for BASIC, which will mean continued growth in its use across manufacturers' lines. Many high schools and colleges are including courses in BASIC in their curricula, and locating competent programmers with commercial experience is becoming easier.

RPG stands for "report program generator." There are several versions around, labeled RPG-I, RPG-II, and (yet to come) RPG-III, but they are variations on the same theme. RPG runs on large mainframe systems and on minicomputers—mainly those from IBM. It began as a shortcut, fill-in-the-blanks style programming language. Then, as users demanded more and more features from it, RPG became increasingly complicated and cumbersome. It executes decently but is somewhat cryptic; however, a fair number of people know the language.

APL stands for "a programming language." It utilizes unusual little symbols to express functions that can be performed on data. Those who know APL are wildly fond of it and rave about its ease and versatility. It is not yet widely available in minicomputers. APL's chief asset seems to be the ease and conciseness with which large, complicated processes can be defined. A small but growing number of programmers know the language.

There are many other languages if one looks for them. Their absence here does not necessarily make them unusable! Do remember, however, that accommodation for the stranger will have to be made at some point and that choosing an esoteric computer language, for whatever current benefits it brings, may cause great difficulties in the future.

Other Ways to Create Computer Programs

At this point, you might feel fairly discouraged by the multitude of languages and the uncertainty of finding appropriate programmers. Fortunately, there have been some heartening developments.

Much of the programming work that goes into creating a business minicomputer system falls into two basic classes:

1. *Programs that "dump" files onto paper.* Such programs, which may add cosmetic touches to the data's appearance on paper, are an element common to all systems. The accounts receivable aged trial balance is a good example of such a process, as the customers' open items are sorted by customer, listed chronologically, and totaled.
2. *Programs that facilitate inquiry into files.* Examples of this type of program are those that permit inspection of a customer's balance or the inventory level of a product.

In both classes of program, the data in the system's files is *unchanged.* The programming involved to produce these programs is not technically difficult, but it takes considerable time to make them attractive and functional. Much work goes into lining up columns and counting out spaces on the printout. In these kinds of programming, it is the housekeeping aspect that represents most of the effort to produce them.

There has been widespread concern over ways to improve the productivity of programmers. Certainly, if programmers did not have to spend time laying out and programming reports, they would have more time to spend on complicated programs. As systems have gotten increasingly inexpensive, the labor cost has *not* shrunk but needs to if such systems are to become widely available. Furthermore, in the case of inquiry programs, what becomes of the user who did not anticipate all the kinds of inquiry he would ever make? He now finds himself with data in his system that would be of use but he has no way to extract it, except by employing a programmer. Many have felt that a user should not be locked away from his own data!

Several farseeing manufacturers, attempting to address these concerns, have developed special "features" for their systems. These special features take the form of a report-producing language that also functions as an ad hoc inquiry facility. The language typically is simple, using terms familiar to the user; since the process would not affect any files, the language can be used freely by the user himself without any adverse effects on his data. This means that the user himself, without programmer assistance, has the ability to draw additional reports from his system. He can also make inquiries about the data in his system, essentially asking his system questions not anticipated at the time of the design of his system and consequently not programmed! For example, let's assume that a system is designed to take orders for the company's product from all over the country and that the zip code of the ship-to is one of the facts collected in the process, as is the proposed method of shipping the goods, e.g., via United Parcel Service (UPS). Let's then imagine that the Chicago area UPS drivers go on strike and that all orders to be shipped UPS to the Chicago area need to be rerouted. You might think this an unusual and probably an unanticipated need for data for a computer system, but this is a true story! With the ability to draw a special report, based upon data already in the system, and without programmer assistance, the user solved his problem literally by asking the system to select and list all unshipped orders that were to have been sent via UPS to destinations with zip codes starting with 606. Management then knew the magnitude of its problem and, armed with the list, set about making alternate arrangements for the orders involved.

Features such as this go by various names. Most utilize a "dictionary" concept, whereby a dictionary of terms is set up for each file on the system, defining the fields in use. The user employs these terms (and must spell them the same way they are shown in the dictionary!), together with a choice of verbs ("list," "sort," etc.) and a few simple syntax requirements to form requests to the system. A request could be phrased "List orders with shipvia 'UPS' and with zipcode beginning with '606.'" Usually the dictionary is established either by a programmer or by someone familiar with the contents of the files. Lists of permissible terms would be made available to all potential users and inquirers. Courses in the contents of the files and the syntax requirements of the request language can be given to various members of the user staff, so that a widespread group of personnel can feel that the system is a resource available to them. With proper management support, a system with a report-generating inquiry feature can open the data in the computer to the entire company!

If a system with features such as these is within your means, *do* give thought to its potential in your company. The abilities described above will lessen your long-term dependence upon programmers, make your system more flexible, versatile, and useful, and perhaps enable you to create a useful tool for a large number of people at your company.

CHAPTER FIVE

The Mystique of Programming

Understanding programming is an important element in understanding computers in general. Once you remove the mystique from programming, the aura of programmers will disappear and you will feel more comfortable picking them, working with them, and judging their work.

What Kind of a Job Is Programming?

Programming is an intermediate level job. Higher level work is done by the people who precede programmers, the "analysts." Systems analysts arrive first on the scene and block out the major tasks that the computer system will and will not do. They determine the overall functions to be performed by the components of the system, the nature and contents of the files involved, and the jobs to be accomplished by the programs to be written. They may go so far as to diagram the logic to be followed by individual programs. At any rate, theirs is the job of designing the system itself. It is the programmer who implements the design. A fair analogy is that of architect and contractor. The architect designs the structure, leaving instructions in the form of blueprints and plans. The contractor translates the plans and blueprints into reality. In much the same way, the programmer translates the intentions of the analyst into computer code and creates a program.

Normally, programmers who do well, and gain some applications expertise, are promoted to analyst level jobs.

What Qualifications Does a Programmer Need?

Almost without exception, people who don't understand computers believe that one has to be good at math to be good at programming. This is (fortunately) not the case. What is needed is the ability to do logical, detailed thinking. At one point music (and especially counterpoint) majors were very much sought after as potential programmers!

If one were to divide the world into two classes, word-people and number-people, thus separating the people who would rather write a story from those who feel at home with a calculator, probably the number-people alone would program computers. But it is the logical, problem-solving capabilities of these individuals that would enable them to program computers, not the ability to do complex calculus or trigonometry (unless, of course, the application itself, such as calculating rocket trajectories, required those aptitudes).

The logical turn of mind is not necessarily acquired in college. Many programmers do well without a college education. This is not to say that it is easy to find a good programming job without the degrees that employers may demand, as a number of constraints are imposed by the job market itself.

Certain personal characteristics also can contribute to success or failure in programming. Programming can be a very *frustrating* occupation! A good programmer needs a great deal of patience, a high tolerance for annoyance and frustration, and a good stomach lining! A person who finds it unbearable to have things go wrong on an unexpected basis will *not* enjoy a career in programming.

Most employers of large numbers of programmers give aptitude tests to prospective programmers or programmer-trainees. These tests, which are similar to mathematics and logic college boards, test for the ability to make logical deductions and to form clear concepts and ideas. Employers rarely give psychological tests to see whether the individual is mentally suited to programming. For the most part, the salary level is not significant enough to warrant an expensive battery of psychological tests from the employer's point of view. Also, the employer knows from experience that a certain amount of "natural selection" will occur: people who are not well suited to programming are likely not to do well at and not to enjoy programming. Many people have given a programming career a try and abandoned it later because of lack of satisfaction and success.

Programmers Draw Those Funny Pictures

The funny pictures programmers draw are "flowcharts." A good programmer learns to draw and to appreciate flowcharts early in his career.

The foundation of programming is the breaking down of the function to be performed into a large number of small and discrete pieces. Once the function has been dissected into all of its parts, the logical processes to be performed can easily be determined. Flowcharting is enormously helpful in laying out the pieces and processes and figuring out their relationships to one another.

The figures and shapes used to draw flowcharts tend to put one off. Programmers usually trace the shapes from a plastic guide called a "programming template." The mystery of the shapes is lessened if you get a chance to inspect the envelope that the programming template comes in. All of the shapes and their uses are explained on the cover of the envelope! Really, the basic shapes are very simple (see page 54). There are many more figures, but knowledge of these basic figures will enable you to read most flowcharts with ease. Almost anything that occurs for some logical reason can be flowcharted. The example on page 55 is a flowchart of the steps performed by a man getting up and going to work!

Can you tell from the flowchart under what conditions the wife gets a goodbye kiss? Note that unless she cooks breakfast, she doesn't get kissed even if she's on her honeymoon! I hope this flowchart, although a bit tongue-in-cheek, is reassuring in its simplicity and clarity. A flowchart of a computer problem should be no more confusing, assuming that you are familiar with the application being programmed.

Flowcharts are useful for several purposes. First, they allow the process to be dissected into its smallest elements, which aids clear thinking about the processing that must be performed. Often, the effort of creating a flowchart for a given problem will point out the solution. Second, the flowchart is a handy way of communicating the desired steps to the person who must implement them. Analysts will often prepare a flowchart of the processing that

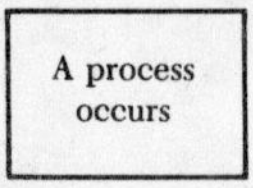

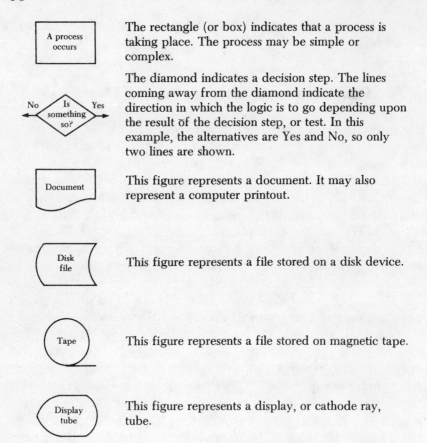

The rectangle (or box) indicates that a process is taking place. The process may be simple or complex.

The diamond indicates a decision step. The lines coming away from the diamond indicate the direction in which the logic is to go depending upon the result of the decision step, or test. In this example, the alternatives are Yes and No, so only two lines are shown.

This figure represents a document. It may also represent a computer printout.

This figure represents a file stored on a disk device.

This figure represents a file stored on magnetic tape.

This figure represents a display, or cathode ray, tube.

is to take place in a program and turn the flowchart over to the programmer, who codes the program (that is, creates it in programming language). If the flowchart is clear, much verbal communication can be avoided, along with the confusion and misunderstandings that can arise through verbal instructions. Third, the flowchart aids the programmer in testing (debugging) his program, as he can compare the desired results on the flowchart at each logical step with the actual results produced by the program when it has been written and run. Fourth, the flowchart serves as an excellent means of documentation once the program has been completed, as it lays out the intentions and logic of the program in simple terms for subsequent reference.

Beware of the programmer who says he doesn't need flowcharts. He may think he doesn't, although he is denying himself the benefits that they can provide, but you *do* need them!

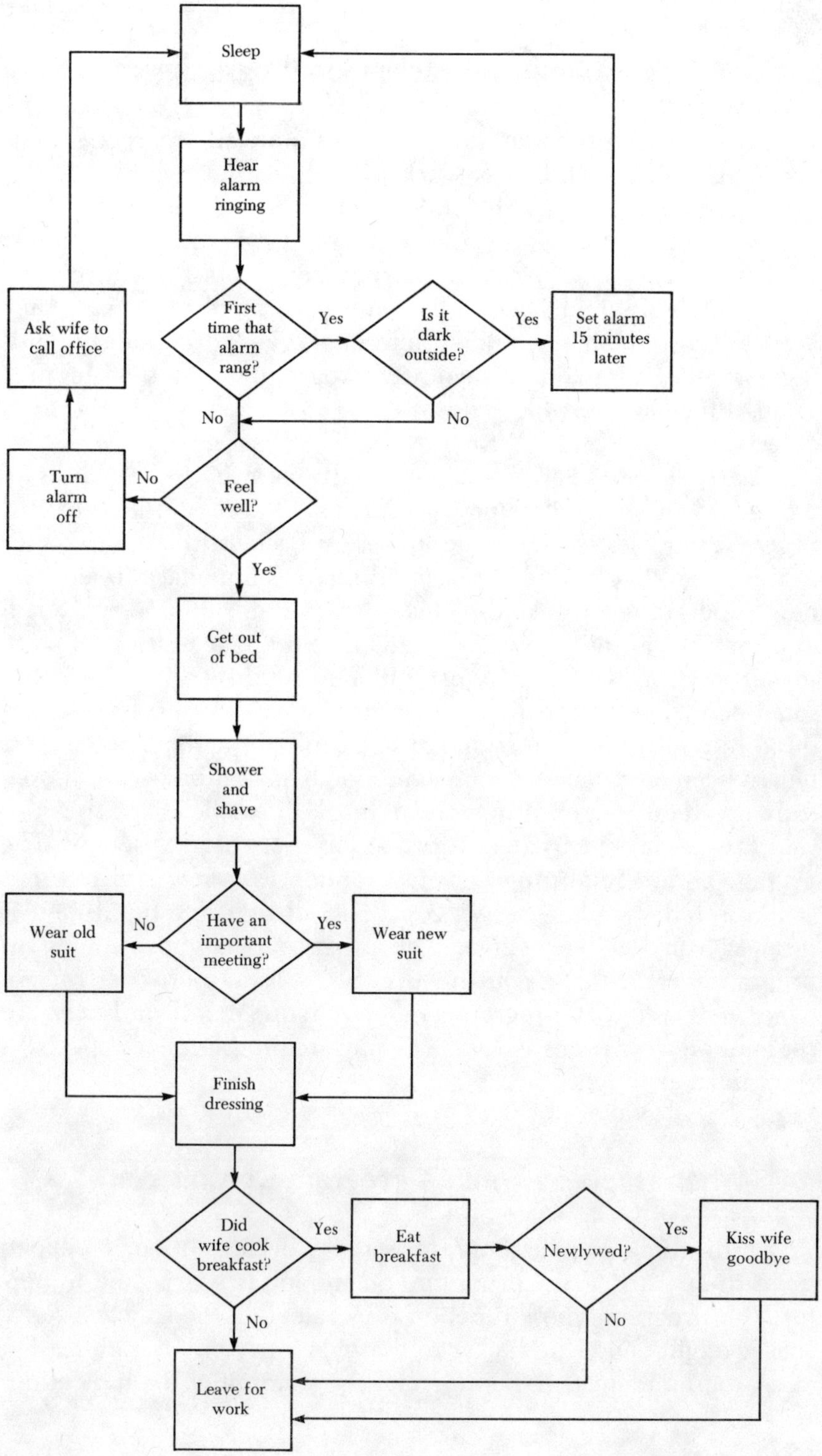
Sleep
Hear alarm ringing
First time that alarm rang?
Yes
Is it dark outside?
Yes
Set alarm 15 minutes later
No
No
Ask wife to call office
Turn alarm off
No
Feel well?
Yes
Get out of bed
Shower and shave
Wear old suit
No
Have an important meeting?
Yes
Wear new suit
Finish dressing
Did wife cook breakfast?
Yes
Eat breakfast
Newlywed?
Yes
Kiss wife goodbye
No
No
Leave for work

The Growing Up Process for Programmers

Almost every programmer goes through a maturation process in his personal attitudes about his work. Some never evolve to be adult programmers but retain the childish attitudes they started with.

In the beginning stages of learning to program, programmers tend to be enormously clumsy, struggling to master the rules of grammar, logic, and syntax of whatever computer language they are learning. Much as a student pilot makes dreadful bouncy landings when learning to fly, the novice programmer often writes programs that have terrible (and often so ridiculous as to be funny) defects.

Later, as proficiency is acquired, the clumsiness is replaced by a tremendous feeling of euphoria and delight at mastering the computer. Having gotten some success under his belt, the programmer at this stage, like the newly licensed pilot, is a menace to all! The new programmer thinks that his work is accurate and masterful and that he can do no wrong. He is casual about testing his work for, after all, it is wonderful, isn't it? During this period, he will at some point have a dreadful experience, which should serve to remind him of his human frailties. The same thing happens to most newly licensed pilots, who at some point have a bad scare (hopefully not fatal) which brings them "back to earth," so to speak!

Programming, by definition, involves numerous details. The average commercial program may contain as many as fifty thousand discrete details. *Nobody* gets them all right the first time—it just isn't physically possible. The programmer who assumes his program is error-free is courting disaster. It is far more constructive to *assume that the program does not work at all and then by thorough testing prove it does.* The mature programmer knows this from hard experience.

When Happens When a Program Doesn't Work?

The indications that a program is not working properly depend upon the nature of the program and the job it is expected to perform. A program whose function is to calculate the trajectory of a rocket might cause the rocket to crash, a fairly obvious indication of a program defect! In commercial programming, the indications are not necessarily so dramatic, although "explosions" have been known to occur in offices where computers caused difficulties.

Traditionally program defects have been called "glitches" or, more commonly, bugs; the process of finding and correcting such defects, debugging. History may not have recorded the original reason for the use of the word "bug," but it is quite appropriate. Program bugs, like cockroaches in the kitchen, hide; they choose their own time and place to venture forth. Only the patient and vigilant have a chance to eradicate them. Even then, the process of battling one bug may allow another bug to go unnoticed.

There are several general categories of program bug. Bear in mind that no bugs are good, but some bugs are worse than others!

Cosmetic bugs are present when the program is actually doing the right thing but expressing it in a sloppy or inaccurate way. For example, two columns on a report may be printed too close together so that the last digit in the leftmost column is cut off—"truncated," in computer terminology. Cosmetic bugs are relatively simple to fix and occur on a consistent basis.

Bugs in processing normal data occur when a mistake is made in specifying the way a calculation or process is performed. An example might be the calculation of sales tax. The faulty placement of a decimal point might result in a 60 percent rather than a 6 percent tax. This kind of bug will produce the wrong (ten times too big) tax on every occasion and should be relatively easy to identify and correct.

Bugs in program logic are indicated when the program does the right thing but at the wrong time (or, conversely, the wrong thing at the right time) through an error in the logical construction of the program, as, for example, in a program that calculated sales tax for customers classified nontaxable. This type of error is also consistently present, although the relationship between the customer's tax status and the amount of tax charged must be identified before the problem can be recognized. In other words, the tax amounts charged will look correct and reasonable and the fact that the customer should not have been charged tax may not be immediately apparent. Bugs like this are more difficult to identify but straightforward to correct.

A major cause of program bugs is the programmer's failure to anticipate all potential situations with which his program may have to cope. We can categorize such bugs as *inabilities to handle unusual situations.* One dreadful example of such a bug is an accounts payable check writing program that wrote checks for vendors who *owed the company a refund or a merchandise exchange.* The seasoned programmer *assumes the worst* about the data coming into his program, whatever their source. Particularly in the case of interactive systems, the programmer must assume that every conceivable kind of error will at some point be made by the (very human) operators. The well-written program tests every piece of data for reasonability and validity at every opportunity. Problems caused by this kind of bug are much more difficult to identify because they will not occur often and will be the result of an unusual event that may have gone unnoticed when it happened.

How Can I Tell a Good Programmer from a Bad One?

If you are going to be affected by the quality of the programming on your system, you should by all means assert the right to interview the programmer(s) who may be involved. Very few potential users ask to do this, probably feeling that they wouldn't know what questions to ask and wouldn't understand the answers. Obviously, a user unfamiliar with computers should not attempt a technical discussion with a programmer lest exactly that situation result. But there is no reason why the user cannot question the programmer in order to try to gauge his programming maturity. Here are some questions you could ask:

"Do your programs require much testing?" "No" should make you dubious.

"Whose fault is it if the operator keys bad data?" A seasoned programmer will accept the blame for bad data his program failed to catch.

"Do you work using flowcharts?" "No" here should end the interview!

"Please rate these qualities from high to low:

1. Program was written in minimum time.
2. Program took up least space in machine.
3. Program executed in least amount of time.
4. Program could never be made to fail under any conditions.
5. Program had impeccable documentation.

The experienced programmer will give higher ratings to numbers 4, 5, and 3, and less importance to numbers 1 and 2.

A Little Programming Test

This test will sound ridiculous both to you and to the persons to whom you assign it! It is deceptively difficult; few people can pass it in a short period of time. Ask for the best commercial programmer available and tell the following story:

> I would like a program that would produce personalized wrapping paper for people to wrap gifts in. This wrapping paper will have a specially personalized message printed on it. I would like to key the message into the keyboard. It will not exceed forty characters. I would like the wrapping paper to print out on the printer, with each line offsetting the message one character to the left in order to make an attractive slanting design.

You can even show the programmer a picture of what you want, which is (assuming you key "Happy Birthday Aunt Claudia" as the text):

```
UNT CLAUDIA             HAPPY BIRTHDAY AUNT CLAUDIA             HAPP
NT CLAUDIA             HAPPY BIRTHDAY AUNT CLAUDIA             HAPPY
T CLAUDIA             HAPPY BIRTHDAY AUNT CLAUDIA             HAPPY
 CLAUDIA             HAPPY BIRTHDAY AUNT CLAUDIA             HAPPY B
CLAUDIA             HAPPY BIRTHDAY AUNT CLAUDIA             HAPPY BI
LAUDIA             HAPPY BIRTHDAY AUNT CLAUDIA             HAPPY BIR
AUDIA             HAPPY BIRTHDAY AUNT CLAUDIA             HAPPY BIRT
UDIA             HAPPY BIRTHDAY AUNT CLAUDIA             HAPPY BIRTH
DIA             HAPPY BIRTHDAY AUNT CLAUDIA             HAPPY BIRTHD
IA             HAPPY BIRTHDAY AUNT CLAUDIA             HAPPY BIRTHDA
A             HAPPY BIRTHDAY AUNT CLAUDIA             HAPPY BIRTHDAY
             HAPPY BIRTHDAY AUNT CLAUDIA             HAPPY BIRTHDAY
            HAPPY BIRTHDAY AUNT CLAUDIA             HAPPY BIRTHDAY A
           HAPPY BIRTHDAY AUNT CLAUDIA             HAPPY BIRTHDAY AU
          HAPPY BIRTHDAY AUNT CLAUDIA             HAPPY BIRTHDAY AUN
         HAPPY BIRTHDAY AUNT CLAUDIA             HAPPY BIRTHDAY AUNT
        HAPPY BIRTHDAY AUNT CLAUDIA             HAPPY BIRTHDAY AUNT
       HAPPY BIRTHDAY AUNT CLAUDIA             HAPPY BIRTHDAY AUNT C
      HAPPY BIRTHDAY AUNT CLAUDIA             HAPPY BIRTHDAY AUNT CL
     HAPPY BIRTHDAY AUNT CLAUDIA             HAPPY BIRTHDAY AUNT CLA
    HAPPY BIRTHDAY AUNT CLAUDIA             HAPPY BIRTHDAY AUNT CLAU
   HAPPY BIRTHDAY AUNT CLAUDIA             HAPPY BIRTHDAY AUNT CLAUD
  HAPPY BIRTHDAY AUNT CLAUDIA             HAPPY BIRTHDAY AUNT CLAUDI
 HAPPY BIRTHDAY AUNT CLAUDIA             HAPPY BIRTHDAY AUNT CLAUDIA
HAPPY BIRTHDAY AUNT CLAUDIA             HAPPY BIRTHDAY AUNT CLAUDIA
APPY BIRTHDAY AUNT CLAUDIA             HAPPY BIRTHDAY AUNT CLAUDIA
PPY BIRTHDAY AUNT CLAUDIA             HAPPY BIRTHDAY AUNT CLAUDIA
```

Ten minutes to program this problem is an acceptable score. You may find someone rare who can do it in five. Far more common will be failure after as much as half an hour! This is *not* an unreasonable test and will help isolate novice programmers from truly competent ones. At the very least, you will test your ability to communicate with the programmer and will probably find some who do not understand what you want even after multiple explanations. A communications gap with the programmer is a poor beginning. *This test is useful.*

Special Considerations in Programming Interactive Minicomputer Systems

This selection involves specific issues with which the programmer has to concern himself. Although the ordinary businessperson will not likely ever to have to cope with these issues himself, it is important for several reasons that he be aware of their existence. First, his working relationship with programmers and analysts is likely to be better if he has more understanding of the problems they face. That's human nature! Second, he may become involved in the joint creation of a programming specification once he has selected his vendor. These concepts should be discussed and included as basic ground rules in programming specifications. A better system will result.

The programmer bears a lot of responsibility for the successful operation of an interactive minicomputer system. This is because the system is generally intended for operation by relatively untrained people. The program is the only thing standing between the operator and bad information entering the system! Thus, the programmer has to take a *defensive posture*, trying to anticipate all the things that might go wrong and preparing a way to handle each of them. Sooner or later, according to the computer maxim called Murphy's law, "If Something Can Go Wrong, It Will." Following this set of guidelines can save an untold amount of grief later.

1. *Assume that the operator is a gorilla* and will key the wrong thing at every opportunity. If the desired response is a zip code, test that the code indeed consists of five numbers and ask

for rekeying if it does not. If the entry is supposed to be the tax rate for a given state, check that the state exists in a state table and then test the tax rate entered against the largest valid rate you know. If numeric digits are to be entered, check that the entry contains no alphabetic characters. If a date is to be entered, check all its parts for reasonableness. The quality of a system depends upon the quality of the data it produces. Another computer maxim, "Garbage in, garbage out," is *so* true. By preventing mistakes from entering the system, you will improve the quality of the output.

2. *Give the operator lots of assistance* by providing a meaningful dialogue of prompts and error messages. Be consistent with terms by calling the same facts and functions by the same names throughout the system. Be specific about the nature of the requests to the operator. The error message "Zip code must have five numeric digits. Please rekey" is much more meaningful than "Error. Rekey." Attention to details such as these will result in a system that requires less intensively trained operators who will make fewer errors through lack of understanding about the system and again will contribute to a higher quality of data in the system.
3. *Assume that the line printer will malfunction during every job.* This advice may seem a bit bizarre but the plain fact is that minicomputer printers are less expensive and generally less reliable than those used on mainframe computers. Making this assumption usually means that programs should be able to reprint part or all of any printed output on demand. This also means that *posting of files should not take place* during print programs. Since the program may have to be rerun because of printer failure, double posting would result. It makes far more sense to have the print program run and to ask the operator at the end whether the report printed satisfactorily. If not, the report can be rerun or restarted with no ill effects. Once the response is yes, a posting program should follow. The printer obviously will not fail on each occasion the program is run; far from it. Where it does malfunction, however, a system that easily copes with the problem will more than pay for itself in the long run.
4. *Assume that multiple users will want to perform every function at the same time.* Minicomputer systems usually have several terminals. Typically there will be common customer,

inventory, and accounts receivable files accessible through each of the terminals. The system designer and the programmer must concern themselves with the problem of multiple users, simultaneously wanting to affect the same data in the system, for sooner or later this will occur. An example may help clarify my point.

> The Gooseneck Lamp Company has a minicomputer system that handles order entry and inventory control functions. Model 100 is the biggest selling gooseneck lamp; there are 200 currently in stock and available for shipment. The computer has a record in the inventory file for Model 100 indicating an on-hand quantity of 200. Two order entry clerks, each at his own terminal, have received orders for Model 100 lamps; the first is for 125 lamps and the second is for 85 lamps.
>
> Operator A enters his order for 125 lamps. The system sees an on-hand quantity of 200 and informs operator A that there is sufficient stock to ship the order. During the (short) interval between the time that operator A is shown the quantity of 200 and the time that operator A reserves 125 for his customer, operator B attempts to order 85 lamps for *his* customer. If the system were to permit him to access the current on-hand quantity, it would be 200 at that instant, certainly adequate to cover his order for 85. In fact, there are only 75 lamps available, which will be known to the system as soon as operator A has completed his transaction. For this reason, it is essential to "lock out" (prevent from accessing) operator B until operator A has completed his transaction. In general, *users intending to change data ought to control that data until their changes are complete. Other users should be queued to wait until the data is fully updated before being given access to it.*

5. *Assume that each function may be interrupted by a mechanical failure.* Power failures do occur and are not in the habit of giving warning! For those jobs with operator interaction, it will generally be fairly obvious what was going on when the interruption occurred. The same is true for jobs that produce printed output. For jobs that run unattended and post files, it is wise to prepare for this contingency by running the job in a predictable (and thus restartable) way. For example, a job that posts the customer file might operate on customers sorted

in name sequence. Also, post the progress of the program on the screen while it is running. In this way, if the power fails when the screen indicates that the program is processing Mr. Schwartz, it is easy to know where to restart and how many customers must be processed to finished the job. Posting the progress of a program that runs without assistance is a good idea anyway as it gives those who are running the system the reassurance that the program is indeed functioning! Sometimes it is very hard to tell whether a program is running. It also gives the operator a way to predict roughly when the job will finish.

If the guidelines given here sound like common sense, that is no coincidence. Good programming relies on common sense and the benefits that experience brings.

CHAPTER SIX

The Care and Feeding of Minicomputers

We can all feel fortunate that the care required for today's minicomputers is very much simpler than that required for the early computers. In the pioneering days of computing, computers needed about as much attention as we might now associate with the construction of a space rocket! Since their memories consisted of thousands of vacuum tubes, the early computers created a great deal of heat, which had to be dissipated by enormous air-conditioning systems. The numerous cables that supplied power to the tubes necessitated raised floors. The equipment also took up vast amounts of space; many people, myself included, actually went *inside* a computer. Temperature, humidity, and air cleanliness were all aspects of the computer's operating environment that had to be carefully controlled, at substantial expense. And the computer's keepers really did wear white lab coats!

Today, the businessperson who is interested in a minicomputer fortunately does not have to go to such trouble and expense. But what does he have to do in the way of care and feeding to keep his minicomputer operating well?

What Goes into Today's Computer Room?

Today's computer concepts generally place the computer in the area with the people who will be using it. Although a formal computer room is not really required with today's smaller, cheaper computers, many companies still have a computer room, for several reasons. First, the line printer does make the kind of noise that a lot of people would not appreciate in their immediate vicinity on a permanent basis; placing the line printer behind closed doors can solve this problem. The disk drives function more reliably if placed out of the main flow of personnel traffic—and away from smokers—as dust and smoke particles tend to cause difficulties with delicate equipment over time. Also, having a specific placement for the more expensive components, the central processor, disk drives, and printer, makes their physical security easier to control. The computer room may also be the logical place to store paper, forms, and supplies necessary to operate the system. Finally, some manufacturers require that certain devices be physically close to each other, usually the printer and the central processor. For all of these reasons, companies still tend to have computer rooms, even with minicomputers. The terminals, however, are frequently placed outside the computer room on the desks of the principal users and operators. Often, however, one terminal is located in the computer room for system operations.

How Is the Computer Room Prepared?

The computer room for today's minicomputer will rarely need a raised floor, as there are fewer cables to accommodate. With most arrangements of the hardware, there is sufficient space in an area where no one needs to walk, usually behind the devices, to lay the cables on the floor.

The room may very well need auxiliary air-conditioning, as the devices that are in the room together will produce a fair amount of heat during normal operations. The amount of air-conditioning needed will depend on the number and nature of the devices used. The largest producers of heat are usually the disk drives. It will depend also upon the air circulation in the computer room.

Each manufacturer makes available a document outlining all the physical specifications and environmental requirements for each piece of hardware it manufactures. This document is usually called a "physical planning guide" or "physical installation manual" or something like that. Included are the ranges of temperature and humidity acceptable for normal operations and the number of BTUs of heat that will be produced per hour for each device. With this information, and with the help of a person who is knowledgeable about air-conditioning and the options available in your location, it should be possible to calculate what accommodations your computer needs. Frequently, a window unit or an extra duct and fan in the ceiling provide enough additional cooling power to dissipate the heat and maintain a proper operating environment. Fortunately, today's systems generally operate best at the same temperature and humidity as people do!

Another aspect that must be considered is the system's electrical supply. The manufacturers' guides usually specify that the entire minicomputer system be placed on its own dedicated circuit so that coffee pots, adding machines, copiers, and other electrical equipment will not interfere with the quality of the system's power. Even if such interference is prevented with a dedicated line, the system may suffer from electrical deviations known as "spikes," "surges," and "brownouts," all names for irregularities in the power supply. These irregularities may come directly from the power source, as is common in large metropolitan areas, particularly in older buildings. Most users can do little more than complain to their local utility when brownouts occur, as few users have the political clout to force the utility to supply steady power!

There are devices that can control, or damp out, irregularities in the power supply. The cheaper devices, known as "voltage regulators," can suppress harmful excesses of power that would damage a computer system. When power is continually too low, devices called "uninterruptible power supply systems" (abbreviated UPS systems) can provide extra power and keep a system running. Voltage regulators come in different sizes and prices but most are affordable to the minicomputer user who has an electrical problem. An uninterruptible power supply system can be more costly than a small minicomputer system! Few minicomputer users find them cost-justifiable, as they would be in a system that absolutely had to be functioning at all times, such as an airline reservation system.

The potential user should obtain the manufacturer's specifications and then discuss the electrical requirements of the system with a trusted person who is knowledgeable about the kind of power supply he can expect in his location. If there are already known problems with the quality of the power, a voltage recorder can be placed on the line for several weeks. This device measures and records the quality of the power and can provide enough information to determine whether voltage regulation is required and if so what kind.

Many users elect to try their system without a voltage

regulator and find that the system operates without problems. If problems occur, they usually are in the nature of the machine's turning itself off when inappropriate power occurs, as most systems have been engineered to shut themselves down without loss of data in that event. If power supply is a continual problem, the decision can be made to record the voltage and obtain the appropriate voltage regulation equipment. It is important that the user have a qualified and trusted electrical advisor who can obtain the voltage recording equipment, interpret the results, and, if necessary, recommend the proper voltage regulation equipment. The manufacturer's staff may be able to provide some assistance in these areas but will be unlikely to be able or willing to provide all of these services on a timely basis.

What Do the Terminals Need?

Each terminal needs to be plugged into an ordinary wall socket for its own electical power. The manufacturer may or may not require that the wall socket be part of the dedicated circuit for the computer itself. The terminal will also need to be cabled to the central processor. The cable may be run down to floor level and covered with a protective sheathing if the area has foot traffic. Frequently such cables are run to the ceiling and travel above the ceiling panels to the computer room, as they can travel a more direct route above the ceiling. There is usually a limit to the length of cable used to connect the terminal to the central processor, as the transmitted signal becomes too weak over too great a cable distance. This maximum will vary from one manufacturer to the next but is rarely less than 400 or more than 1,000 feet. The details will be found in the physical installation manual.

Terminals can be operated at greater distances, usually through telephone lines.

Does the Computer Need a Periodic Checkup?

Yes, it does. Manufacturers and users have found that preventive maintenance is cost-effective. Most users are willing to give up several expected hours a month rather than suffer malfunctions and lost processing time (called "down time"), on an unexpected basis. Murphy's law also means that the computer will break down at the very worst possible time for the user!

Preventive maintenance procedures differ from one system to the next. They generally involve changing the filters on the disk drives and running diagnostic tests on the devices and memory. These tests are intended to exercise all aspects of operation in order to detect irregularities. Some of today's systems even keep track of the number of failures they experience in the course of normal operations. A failure might be the inability to read a disk record within the first ten tries, for example. At preventive maintenance time, the repairperson (whose high salary justifies his being called a "field engineer") can inspect these various error counts and determine whether repairs or adjustments are in order. Occasionally, small problems such as printer hammer adjustments or screen contrast adjustments that do not merit a service call by themselves are corrected during preventive maintenance.

Most minicomputers are fairly reliable. A frequent problem, however, is that terminal keys stick or fail to function. Users who ban food and drink near the keyboards have far fewer such problems!

A log book of the maintenance procedures that were performed and the parts replaced is generally kept for each device by the field engineer or other maintenance personnel. The user is also well advised to keep his own log of all machine malfunctions, service calls, and down time. In this way, the total and average amounts of time lost through machine problems can be recorded. These records assist in planning machine operations and preventive maintenance. They may also form the basis of a complaint letter to the manufacturer! Very often, good records of hardware problems enable a mystery to be solved later, when perhaps a transaction is found to be missing or not to make sense.

Computer Security Precautions

The arrangements we have discussed so far are intended to provide a physical environment that will keep your system running as much of the time as possible. It is also necessary to create a *secure* environment for your system.

Fire is always a threat. Accordingly, the computer room should have carbon dioxide fire extinguishers in strategic locations. Non–carbon dioxide extinguishers should *not* be used as they can cause even greater permanent damage to the system. A switch that breaks the entire electrical circuit for the system should be placed near the door and should be used in the event of an electrical fire involving the system. Staff members should be trained in the use of extinguishers and circuit breakers.

Water damage is also a real possibility in most buildings. Plastic drop cloths should be placed in a convenient location, and the staff should be instructed how to cover the equipment in the event of water flooding.

Even if the computer hardware is totally destroyed, it can always be replaced through insurance, which also should be arranged for by the user. The one element of a computer system that *cannot be obtained anywhere else* is the user's own data. Reconstructing lists of customer names and addresses, current and back orders, accounts receivable, and inventory positions would be virtually impossible, especially if the manual records of the company were also destroyed at the time the computer files were lost. It is critical, then, that the company's data, the one irreplaceable element, be given as much attention as all of the physical equipment.

I have spoken before of "backing up," the process of making copies of all the system's files and programs on a regular basis for security purposes. At least one fairly current set of backup files should be taken off the premises, by which I do not necessarily mean a bank vault. Actually, the use of a bank vault can be counterproductive, as the restricted time during which the vault is usually accessible tends to prevent the backup process from taking place as it should. The simple procedure of an employee's taking a set of files to his home and exchanging them for a new set on a monthly basis satisfies the security objective nicely. Other backup copies are taken daily and weekly but remain on the premises. In the event of damage to all of these, it may be necessary to reconstruct up to one month's activity and data at most, depending upon the timing of the loss. One month of reconstruction is possible, whereas complete reconstruction is not.

Security precautions also include protecting the system against the acts of disgruntled or careless employees. The computer room ought to have a lock and key or other device that limits entry. As normal operating procedure, only authorized personnel who have a need to be present should be permitted in the computer room. Inadvertent destruction must be prevented as well. Programs and procedures that have serious effects on system files must be protected against improper use by demanding security passwords and verification checks before they are run.

CHAPTER SEVEN

What Do Minicomputers Do?

Answering the question "What do minicomputers do?" is similar to trying to describe what cars look like. Just as there are many different shapes, sizes, and colors of car, there are diverse functions performed by minicomputers.

Most minicomputer functions are associated with traditional business activities such as accounts receivable, order entry, and inventory control. But there is no requirement that limits minicomputers to such tasks. One system in Colorado keeps track of cowboys who ride in rodeos and their performances and rankings. A system in Missouri keeps track of the plant and shrub inventory at a cemetery and schedules routes for lawn mowers. Minicomputers can serve as a useful tool for any kind of business.

Today's minicomputer systems have their antecedents in a number of different areas. Some systems have grown out of smaller systems; others are offshoots of larger ones.

An Alternative to Service Bureau Processing

Service bureaus have been a very popular way for users to gain access to computers much larger than ones they would be able to afford alone. With the service bureau concept, many users effectively share the costs of very large mainframe systems.

To process at a service bureau, the user makes an appointment for a block of computer time and appears with his data already prepared (keypunched) for processing. If he is not ready for processing at the appointed time, he has to make another appointment, as there is little flexibility in the schedule at most service bureaus. Should the job run over the allotted block of time, the user may be forced to vacate the system before his job is completed. Another disadvantage is the hassle of transporting data, files, and forms back and forth, although some service bureaus provide clerical work space and storage privileges at varying degrees of cost.

A few service bureaus have established themselves as providers of specialized processing services. These service bureaus offer a measure of programming and processing expertise that the user may not be able to obtain on his own. For example, payroll processing service bureaus include with their computer time up-to-date state, federal, and local tax computations, employee paychecks and W-2 forms at year-end, all required government reports, confidential processing, and pickup and delivery service, all at a very low cost per transaction. Service bureaus that have combined processing on large mainframe computers with data processing expertise generally have maintained their customer bases intact. Many other service bureaus have lost their larger customers to the in-house minicomputer. Once minicomputers became big enough and cheap enough to compete with mainframes, customers welcomed them as a way to do their own processing on their own premises at their own convenience.

An Alternative to Time-sharing

Users of time-sharing computing services also gain access to much larger computers than they could afford by themselves. A time-sharing user normally has some sort of terminal, usually a teletype with a paper tape attachment, at his own location. He prepares his program and data on punched paper tape in advance of being connected to the computer, if possible, as the terminal works without being connected to the computer, as well. He calls the computer through the telephone network and gives an assigned number that identifies him as a valid user of the system. He then shares the computer with the other users who are on the system at the same time. Generally, through a queuing arrangement, he is given the computer's attention at specified intervals (ideally too short to be noticed) and then placed at the bottom of the queue again. The intervals of waiting for the computer's attention vary with the number of other users and the scheme to allocate time among them.

The user can store programs or data within the computer's storage files if he wishes. He is charged for the amount of computer time he has used, the amount of time he is connected to the computer, and the amount of characters of data and programs he has stored during the billing period.

Frequent users of time-sharing services have found crowded processing conditions during the peak demand hours of the day, generally midday. They have found the preparation, handling, and storage of paper tape data and programs to be very inconvenient and storage on the computer to be relatively expensive. The computer processing and connect-time charges are both expensive and difficult to predict and control. The response time can degrade substantially because of peak demand periods and user overloads.

Some time-sharing users have been involved principally in scientific and technical computer processing, which requires a lot of computation but very little input or output activity. Such jobs benefit from the major advantage of time-sharing: access to a computer with a great deal of processing power. They avoid the main disadvantage: clumsy and expensive handling of large amounts of data on the way in and the way out.

Many time-sharing users have migrated toward minicomputers. This is logical since the early minicomputers began with scientific and technical users and employed languages such as FORTRAN and BASIC, which facilitate mathematical programming. Minicomputers had an initial attraction for scientific and technical users. As the peripheral devices that facilitate the handling of large amounts of input and output data became cheaper and more reliable, the minicomputer became attractive to commercial time-sharing users as well.

Another class of user utilized time-sharing services to take advantage of the national and international networks that have been established. Several of the larger time-sharing vendors have established networks in which numerous cities are tied into common computer centers. Making only a local call, a user in Los Angeles can access data placed in a central computer by his office in New York! Companies with offices in diverse geographic locations can thus share data with each other without establishing their own communications networks and without incurring long-distance charges. Of course, the costs of such communications networks are embedded in the time-sharing charges.

Some users with national and international communications requirements such as these have found that they can substitute minicomputers for the terminals at their various locations at a savings over time-sharing charges. The minicomputers collect and pool local data and then transmit it to and exchange it with other minicomputers and central computers at high speeds at different times. The economies available in this kind of conversion depend upon the distances involved and the availability of bulk communications charging arrangements among the locations.

Extensions to Mainframe Computers

Many users have extended the capabilities of their mainframe computers by combining them with minicomputers. The minicomputers are often used as data collection systems, replacing traditional keypunch equipment; they enable the user to prepare his data interactively. The minicomputers are able to obtain files and tables from the mainframe computers automatically and easily, and they guide the operators through the kinds of interactive data entry routines discussed previously. Punched cards can be bypassed completely either by having the minicomputers transmit data directly to the mainframe computer or by recording the data on magnetic tape for later use.

Minicomputers have also been used to extend mainframe computers in ways that are not obvious to the everyday user. Systems with enormous communications networks, such as airline reservations systems, have thousands of users connected to them and process thousands of requests every minute. Minicomputers have been utilized to direct the flow of such messages and requests, effectively fielding them, determining their priority and nature, and directing them to the proper part of the system, thereby relieving the mainframe computer of this effort.

Enhanced Accounting Machines

Minicomputers have found their way into accounting systems as well. Early accounting machines contained complicated gear mechanisms, type bars, and many moving parts. Their circuitry was cumbersome and their functions limited. Some systems incorporated ledger card units. Each ledger card could represent a customer, an inventory item, or some other record to which transactions were to be posted. The operator located the correct card or cards for a given transaction and pulled the card(s) from a tub containing numerous cards. Each card in turn was inserted into the ledger card unit for posting. The card was printed with a line showing the balance before the transaction, the transaction, and the balance afterward. On some systems, the current balance was also recorded on a magnetic strip on the back of the card. The operation was time-consuming and labor-intensive in that a great deal of manual effort was required for the searching and dunking process that accompanied every transaction.

Modern minicomputer systems have obviated the need for ledger cards. Inexpensive disk storage takes the place of the ledger card and can be posted easily and inquired upon with ease. Much operator effort is avoided. Minicomputers have replaced accounting machines to the extent that it is becoming increasingly difficult to find service personnel and parts for early model accounting machines.

Enlarged Calculators

Minicomputer and microcomputer technology has progressed to such a point that some of today's calculators are actually true computers as they have the ability to store programs and data. Special-purpose minicomputers now perform functions previously done manually with the aid of calculators, such as standard statistical and bond amortization calculations.

Intelligent Terminals

As the use of terminals has become widespread, minicomputers have been built into terminals, which then become "intelligent terminals" (yes, the others are called "dumb terminals"!). Such terminals have the ability to perform some editing and logical checking of data on a local basis, thus saving that effort on the part of the mainframe computer to which the terminal is attached. These terminals usually also have the ability to store substantial amounts of data internally, as many as two or four thousand characters in some instances, and can forward this data to the mainframe computer all at one time, thereby reducing processing delays and communications expense.

What Applications Are the Best Candidates for Minicomputers?

In general, the applications that have been the most attractive candidates for computerization have been those with the largest transaction volumes and the greatest flow of repetitive data. These applications traditionally have been those in the accounting and basic recordkeeping areas, such as accounts receivable, accounts payable, general ledger, payroll, and list maintenance. These areas normally have the largest volume of transactions and the highest concentration of clerical effort, offering the greatest possibilities for savings.

Applications that have the most effect on the company's way of doing business are also attractive candidates for computerization. These applications offer opportunities for providing better service to customers, collecting debts faster, and decreasing working capital requirements.

For example, one company was able to take a substantial lead over competitors by mechanizing its order entry and inventory status functions. Order entry clerks were given computer terminals and telephone headsets. As telephone orders came in, the clerk consulted the terminal and was able to tell the customer the expected shipping date of the order. If the product was out of stock, the expected date for fulfillment of the back order was given. The company advertised this customer service, turning a computer application into a marketing coup.

Another company found that the computerization of inventory enabled it to streamline reordering and predict stock levels to the point that it needed much less component inventory on hand in order to avoid shortages. This company was able to convert the assets being used to finance inventory levels into working capital useful in other areas of its operations.

A third company found that by capturing sales information as a by-product of the order entry function, it was able to assist its sales staff enormously. The sales staff for the first time was able to monitor sales, knowing immediately what products were and were not selling and which customers were and were not buying. Using this information, the company found it could greatly improve the productivity of the sales staff, and this productivity boosted sales.

Each of these three examples illustrates a situation in which a computer application had a large effect on company operations. In each case, the decision to computerize did not rest upon the manual effort required to perform the function, for the function was not being performed at all! The computer enabled the company to perform a function that had previously been impossible and that produced favorable bottom-line results.

Other application areas are appealing as well. Many companies do some kind of word processing as they prepare correspondence, sales literature, catalogs, contracts, and other documents. Increasingly, today's small business computers include word processing and text editing software in their packaged programs. Preparation of textual data on a minicomputer is an attractive additional application as it offers several useful features. First, the operator can set up the textual data on a terminal, where it can be visually reviewed and corrected before being printed on paper. Second, paragraphs and sections of text can be stored in the computer and inserted with little effort; documents that will be prepared over and over again with minor modifications can be stored for reuse. Third, large sections of text can be rearranged with a few simple instructions; powerful commands can locate certain occurrences of words or phrases within the text and easily change the words or phrases.

Finally, within each industry there are specialized applications that have become popular candidates for minicomputer applications. For example, computer assisted design and graphics systems have been highly successful in streamlining the drafting process. The most logical place to learn about the advances that minicomputers are making into a particular industry would be that industry's trade shows, where several varieties of specialized minicomputer systems for that industry would no doubt be on display.

CHAPTER EIGHT

Could a Minicomputer Be Used Effectively?

Many businesspeople feel that eventually their business should have a computer. The question to them is not whether but when. They realize that buying a computer prematurely might be a mistake: the computer costs money and requires a substantial amount of effort on the part of management and staff to get it running, straining the company's operations in the process. Accordingly, how does one know when the right time has come to embark on this effort?

There is no easy answer. Merely assembling enough facts on which to base the decision to computerize is a lot of work. In this chapter I discuss some of the potential benefits and costs of a computer system and explore some of the right and wrong reasons for wanting to computerize.

Potential Benefits of a Computer System

Some anticipated benefits are specific and quantifiable.

1. *Improved customer service.* Shipments to customers can be made more quickly and more accurately or otherwise improved in such a way that sales are boosted, expenses lessened, and profits increased.
2. *Improved cash flow.* Receivables are collected more quickly and payables are paid more strategically, resulting in a more advantageous cash flow for the company.

3. *Improved working capital requirements.* Inventory is more closely controlled, shrinkage is lessened, and shortages are minimized, making working capital available for other uses within the company.

Other benefits may be anticipated and may occur but are more difficult to quantify.

4. *Forestalled hiring.* Most non-users have the misconception that they will be able to decrease staff costs with a computer system. Exactly the opposite has usually proven to be the case. Personnel costs rise during the short run because extra positions frequently are required by the new computer. Savings may be realized, but they generally occur fractionally (i.e., the total of different people's responsibilities may be reduced, but not in such a way that any one person's job can be eliminated). These fractional savings are immediately absorbed by functions never performed in the past but now possible The best that can be hoped for is that the company can manage substantial growth without incurring substantial staff increases as a result of computerization. This is a realistic expectation, and has happened frequently. Many companies have been satisfied to do more work for the same expense, if not the same work at less expense.
5. *Better data for management.* Computer systems that are well designed can improve the quality of management information available to a company. Using this improved data for monitoring and forecasting can have a number of beneficial effects, although they are largely indirect and difficult to quantify. For example, sales personnel can be kept up-to-date on the identities of buyers and non-buyers and can target their efforts better. They can also be made aware on an immediate basis of which products are and are not selling well. Development personnel receive feedback on which products are being accepted in the marketplace. Financial personnel can get up-to-date information on the company's receivables, payables, income, and expenses and can manage their resources to better advantage, but information alone will not secure these benefits —it must be acted upon.

6. *Streamlined systems and procedures.* There is an adage that "confusion costs money." Some indirect and long-range benefits may occur as the company revamps its systems and simplifies its procedures in connection with computerization. One of the plain truths that often emerge is that the computer is the *only* place to look for information, whereas previously there might have been a number of sources, including peoples' desks! If the computer system has been designed with efficiency in mind, there will be fewer wasted steps and less duplication of effort.
7. *Improved quality of staff time.* With more information and with streamlined systems and procedures, the quality of the time spent by staff members improves. Research into petty, mundane problems decreases, and time becomes available for consideration of long-range trends and alternatives.

Obviously none of these benefits can be obtained for nothing. Thus, we need to look at the costs of computerizing.

Potential Costs of a Computer System

Some of the costs are obvious and are known in detail at the outset.

1. *Hardware purchase price.* This number receives a great deal of attention. If the hardware is financed or leased, the costs of financing must be added to the purchase price.
2. *Monthly hardware maintenance.* This is the fixed fee charged by the hardware maintenance vendor for the periodic repair and preventive maintenance performed on the hardware. This fee often will be increased at the time of contract renewal. Depending upon the supply of maintenance vendors (usually there are few alternatives), the user may have to accept whatever increase is proposed by the vendor.
3. *Supplies.* Stock paper, preprinted forms, magnetic tape, and disk packs will be recurring costs for the life of the system.
4. *One-time preparation expense.* These expenses are incurred in preparing for the arrival of the computer and include electrical, air-conditioning, carpentry, painting, and telephone

installation costs. They also include furniture, fire extinguishers, and other one-time expenses.

5. *Software purchase price.* If a fixed fee, this charge is known at the outset. If the software is an estimated fee, some adjustment should be made for cost overruns and unforeseen needs, as they frequently occur.
6. *Software maintenance.* This is the fee charged for maintenance of programs after the software warranty has expired. If you have no such arrangement, expect some degree of expense here, for several reasons. First, certain software problems will not become evident until the first year of operation is over! Second, users rarely think of everything they would like in software on the first try and are bound to want extensions, enhancements, and improvements over time. While these costs should be considered on each occasion relative to the benefits they are expected to bring, such expenses will nonetheless occur.
7. *Hardware depreciation.* Many users fail to recognize this item of expense. A qualified accountant will be able to advise the proper conservative rate of depreciation to assume.

Some hidden costs arise even with a successful installation.

8. *Diversion of managerial and supervisory time.* The company staff member in charge of the project will be working almost full-time on it. Other members will be busy with interviews and meetings and will certainly spend less time on normal duties. The computer system vendor may be able to help in quantifying the actual time that will be required, as will conversations with other users.
9. *Retraining of staff.* You may elect to have staff members formally trained in a schoollike environment, or you can phase training over a long period of hands-on operations. In either case, company resources will go into the effort to train staff.
10. *Conversion expense.* Expenses will be incurred in transferring your existing data to the new computer system. You may have to pay for programs to convert your data from other machines and/or hire temporary help or pay overtime to have the data keyed into the system from manual records.
11. *Obsolescense expense.* Occasionally a system brings a great

deal of success to a company, which then experiences a high rate of growth. Unfortunately, the chosen system may not be able to expand to carry the required growth and a newer, bigger system may have to be obtained much earlier than was expected. Attention to capacities at the time of hardware selection is important in preventing this problem, but in some cases company growth may exceed everyone's wildest expectations. Most users accept this cost as the price of success!

If your installation is not entirely smooth and problem-free, there is another, entirely different set of expenses to be borne.

12. *Reprogramming.* Some parts of the system may be deemed unworkable with the twenty-twenty vision of hindsight, and they may have to be completely reprogrammed. Predicting such a development is impossible, so the potential user should beware. For several reasons reprogramming tends to be more expensive than the original job. First, the user is not as likely to be looking for a bargain the second time around. Second, the computer is likely to be operating under live conditions now; assembling the resources necessary to change operations in midstream requires a higher level of expertise, which is usually more expensive.
13. *Delays in business operations.* Production may be delayed because of unforeseen shortages and technical problems, shipping schedules may suffer, orders may be lost or taken incorrectly, cash flow may degrade, and financial statements may be late and not balance. The list of things that can go wrong is endless. The important thing to realize is that your company's success is dependent upon the success of the computerization effort and that *by attempting to computerize you are risking vulnerability.*
14. *Possible loss of customer goodwill.* When customer orders are delayed, filled erroneously, or lost or when billing errors appear on customer statements, you become a problem for the customer and are likely to lose customer goodwill in the process. The actual expense is difficult to quantify but is undesirable in any amount!
15. *Possible loss of company data or of credibility.* When a computer system produces bad data, there can be great damage

to a company's morale and reputation. Suspicion of the accuracy of data leads to multiple data rechecks, increasing employee workloads. Staff members who have to work with shaky or incomplete data quickly become frustrated and discouraged and lose respect for management. Customers who write requesting clarification of transactions and receive no satisfaction also lose confidence quickly.

16. *Data replacement and correction expense.* Most companies are not staffed to cope with the problem of destroyed or damaged data; they are staffed at a level sufficient to cope with current requirements only. Usually, temporary staff has to be brought in to help research and repair problematic data—at extra expense—and in-house supervisory personnel will have to spend time managing this effort.

This last group of expenses is unpleasant to consider. These costs are difficult to predict and quantify, but it is very important that the potential user *be aware* that they may occur and make every effort to prevent them.

Why Do You Want a Computer System?

Here are some common reasons for wanting a computer system and a brief commentary on each.

1. "My biggest competitor has one. I'm afraid he will gain a competitive edge over me if I don't get one, too." Well, the competitor just might be doing you a *big favor.* There is no way of knowing whether he has done his homework and given computerization a lot of careful thought. He may be cutting his own throat, but that doesn't mean you should also! This reason by itself is *not* a good enough basis for getting a computer system.
2. "My business is sick and a computer will fix it." This approach will result in a computerized sick business. Rarely does computerization clean up a mess; usually it causes a computerized mess. If your company is in trouble, it would be wiser to postpone computerization until you tightened controls, installed standards, and generally cleaned house.

3. "A computer will allow me to cut down on staff." The computer rarely allows a decrease in staff expense; at best it permits growth without substantial hiring.
4. "We can try it and see whether it works." Computerization seems to be a one-way street. It is most difficult to abandon a computer system without incurring expense and damage to the company. This kind of reasoning is asking for lots of trouble.
5. "We'll learn about computers while doing it." The time to learn the basics about computers is *not* after the monster arrives. The decision to computerize should be based on a solid understanding of what a computer can and cannot do. This kind of reasoning leads to unrealistic expectations and sure disappointment.

Finally, what are the right reasons? If you can make the statements below with sincerity, you are likely to be ready for your first computer system.

1. "I have analyzed and understand the processes that are performed in each area of my company. I have tried to make manual improvements everywhere possible. I know exactly which processes would benefit from computerization. I know how I would use the manpower freed up by the computer and how much it would profit me." This user has done his homework and has specific expectations and plans for his system.
2. "I have worked out a long-term business plan. I know exactly when and how I would like my company to grow. I know what role I would like the computer to play in this growth."
3. "I have studied the obvious and hidden costs associated with computerization. I realize that I am taking some risk. I have analyzed the potential benefits and feel that my company will be getting a good return on its investment in a computer system."

CHAPTER NINE

Writing a Request for Proposal

The "request for proposal," abbreviated RFP, may also be called the "request for quotation," abbreviated RFQ. Its preparation is the *single most important step* in the process of obtaining and implementing a successful computer system.

What Is an RFP?

The RFP is analogous to the specifications that are commonly drawn up in some industries when preparing to purchase goods and services. The document describes what is needed, the terms under which the purchase can be considered, and the requirements that the goods and services must fulfill. The RFP, which is normally prepared when multiple vendors are being considered, generally asks that the vendors respond with a quotation and/or a proposal. Vendors who do not wish to be considered can decline to respond; those who do respond will be compared with each other. For reasons that will be outlined here, it may make sense to prepare an RFP when only a single vendor is being evaluated.

Why Write an RFP?

There are many reasons why writing an RFP is a good idea. As stated above, the RFP is an integral part of the process of finding and installing a successful computer system. Let us explore the reasons why.

Taking an Active Role in Determining Your Needs

Preparation of an RFP is beneficial in itself. This effort enables a company to take an active role in determining how the new computer system should work. The company that takes advantage of this opportunity finds itself in the position of being able to *declare* what is needed, rather than *ask*. While it takes some effort to educate yourself well enough to be in this position, the long-range benefits are enormous. The simple fact is that *no one understands your business better than you do.*

Companies who would never consider accepting a stranger's advice on how to reorganize their production facilities meekly accept the same sort of advice about their systems and procedures from computer salespeople who are entirely uninformed about their operations. The company is better off making an intelligent buying decision than allowing a sales representative to make an intelligent selling decision!

The first good reason for writing an RFP, then, is that it puts your company in the driver's seat, in control of the situation.

An Opportunity to Review All Your Current Procedures

The investigation that management should make in preparing an RFP is a good education in the company's current systems and procedures. Invariably, the investigation unearths situations in which work is being performed differently from the way management thought, unnecessarily, or not at all! Often the investigation results in improvements that can be implemented immediately at little or no cost.

As each application is reviewed, existing policies and procedures can be questioned. Clerical efforts can be redirected. These activities can and should involve contributions from many staff members. It is important that staff members at all levels feel part of the process of obtaining a computer system and that their contribution is needed. Staff participation at the RFP stage very much improves staff cooperation during implementation.

An Opportunity to Concentrate on Long-term Business Planning

Long-term planning often is postponed in the interests of running a business with its day-to-day problems. In preparing an RFP, management is forced to concentrate on long-term objectives; it must consider planning the company's growth, estimating future transaction volumes, and improving customer service, cash flow, and profitability.

The RFP Makes Dealing with Vendors Easier

It can be very time-consuming to explain your company's policies, goals, procedures, plans, and practices to each potential vendor of computer systems. Inevitably, some vendors get a better tour than others and others miss hearing something important. Some vendors may insist on spending time with your staff, reviewing systems, procedures, forms, and files.

It is far more efficient to give each vendor a substantial RFP to absorb first. Thus each vendor starts with the same base of facts. The vendors' understanding of the job to be done can be fairly compared, as each started with the same base. The quality of questions and comments can be compared as well. Time is saved in giving tours and answering questions, and staff interruptions are minimized.

Vendors Who Know More Charge Less

Vendors have to stay in business, too. They cannot afford to make estimates that fail to reflect the actual amount of work to be performed for a customer. Their risk is even greater if they operate on a fixed fee, or turnkey (a combined price for all hardware and software), basis, for the failure to quote accurately leads directly to a loss for the vendor. Knowing this, you should *expect vendors to price for uncertainty.* When a vendor is given very little information about a job to be done, he tries to fill in what is missing and must inflate the price to cover unknown contingencies. Accordingly, a vendor presented with specific and thorough information will have less need to price for uncertainty.

While the preparation of an RFP may seem like a lot of work, effort, and expense, it rarely fails to improve prices and results.

The RFP Documents the Goals of the System

All systems need documentation; most suffer from not having enough. The RFP provides useful documentation long after the vendor search is completed. It can be given to new staff members to read, as it is a succinct review of the systems and procedures followed prior to computerization. It can be referred to (and will be!) throughout the implementation period. Questions such as "How were we going to handle the wholesale discount?" will continually crop up. Systems planning involves many such decisions. Few people will remember for long every discussion, conclusion, and plan. The RFP is a way to document these decisions.

The RFP Is the Foundation of the Programming Specifications

In many systems, once the vendor is chosen, a programming specification is written by vendor and staff together. This document is based upon the RFP, extending and refining it. For example, where the RFP refers to the creation of a particular report by the system, the programming specification might contain a detailed layout of the report. In addition, the programming specification would describe the report's contents exactly in terms of the sources of the information in the report and would detail the circumstances under which the report would be produced.

The RFP is the starting point for the preparation of the programming specification. Without an RFP, the programming specifications would take a great deal more time and money to produce.

The RFP Prevents Disputes

Disagreements (and they can occur) between vendor and customer can be prevented if the RFP provides good documentation of exactly what was desired by the customer. All the "But you never mentioned . . ." and "I thought I was getting . . ." discussions are nipped in the bud.

A List of Wishes for the Computer Fairy?

The RFP is the place for long-term creative thinking. It is the place to consider the *ideal* computer system, unfettered by machine limitations, human shortcomings, budget constraints, and all the other realities that make implementing systems more difficult than we would like. Acknowledging, of course, that compromises will have to be made, you can use the RFP to ask, "Would it be possible to . . ." and "How long would it take if . . ." and "What would it cost if . . ." Occasionally, some of these musings turn out to be practicable. Computers are peculiar that way: things that seem as though they should be hard are simple, and vice versa.

The RFP can easily become a wish list if this approach is taken too far! It is all too tempting to ask for the best possible system, at the cheapest possible price, in the shortest possible time. These three goals will always conflict with each other, and realistic choices among them have to be made. Management must sincerely try to set for itself goals that are accurate, clearly defined, realistic, and compatible.

There is no harm in including some of the "What if . ." things in the RFP. State that you are uncertain of their cost-effectiveness, and that you would like prospective vendors to price them separately. Then a sensible decision can be made about their inclusion in the final system.

What Should the RFP Contain?

Some basic points should be covered in order for the RFP to fulfill its objectives. The outline and sample texts given here have proven useful and are presented as a guide and a checklist. This is not to say that other arrangements would not suffice. The prose is not sacred and could easily be rewritten to suit another's taste. The main idea is that these issues be addressed.

First, the RFP should have a cover letter explaining when a response is expected and to whom questions can be directed. The letter should include an acknowledgment page, upon which the vendor acknowledges receipt of a confidential document, and a table of contents for ease of reference.

Requirements pertaining to the overall system (as opposed to a single application) can be grouped into a general requirements section that discusses hardware, software, and system functions.

A review of the company's background and the nature of its current business is usually extremely helpful to vendors in providing an overall understanding of the system's future environment and the objectives to be met.

Each application should be discussed separately and its goals and objectives identified. Some attention should be given both to describing how the application is currently being performed (if it is) and to enumerating changes envisioned with computerization. A brief description of the data elements that go into the process and the reports and end products that emerge should also be included.

The volumes of records and transactions can be listed with each of the applications to which they pertain of they can be grouped together in a final section on system files, transaction counts, and statistics. This section may list the data that should be included in various system files.

Sample of Cover Letter

The Gooseneck Lamp Company
21 Downy Lane
New York, New York, 10017
212-321-0098

January 4, 1980

Mr. John Best
Best Systems Ever, Inc.
24 Paradise Avenue
New York, New York 10017

Dear Mr. Best:

The attached document represents our company's Request for Proposal for a business computer system. Proposals should be received at our offices no later than 3 P.M. Monday, February 4, 1980. Questions may be directed to our controller, George Acedigit, at this address.

Please sign the Acknowledgment of Confidentiality on page 2 upon receipt of this document and return it immediately to the address indicated.

We very much look forward to receiving your response.

Sincerely yours,

Bob Jones

Bob Jones
President

The Cover Letter

The purpose of the cover letter is to introduce the RFP to the recipient, establish how and when a response should be made, and identify the person to whom questions should be directed. You can see from the sample letter shown on page 92 that a month was allowed for the vendors to prepare their responses. This will usually be ample time for all the vendors but one, who will present a very credible excuse and ask for an extension. Be prepared to give the extension.

Acknowledgment of Confidentiality

This document is to be signed as soon as the vendor receives the RFP and returned to the company. It advises the company that the document was indeed received and sets a tone of respect for the confidentiality of the company's business procedures. This may seem to some to be an unnecessary precaution, but it causes no harm or difficulty and in some instances could prevent serious problems.

Sample

Acknowledgment of Confidentiality

Return to:
Mr. George Acedigit
Controller
The Gooseneck Lamp Co.
21 Downy Lane
New York, New York 10017

The undersigned confirms receipt of specifications from The Gooseneck Lamp Co. for the purpose of preparing a proposal for a computer system and acknowledges that all information contained herein shall be kept in the strictest confidence and shall not be divulged to persons other than those who are responding to this request.

____________________ ____________________
Date By

____
Title

The Table of Contents

This page outlines the contents of the document and indicates the page numbers upon which the various subjects are covered.

Sample

Table of Contents

Overall System Requirements

This section discusses the premises, or ground rules, upon which the company wishes to base its relationship with the chosen vendor. While it is not mandatory to include such a section, experience has shown that to announce such premises in advance may prevent unpleasant situations in the future. The company in the sample determined the following to be the relationship they wanted:

Sample

The company wishes to minimize its financial risks insofar as possible. Therefore, it wishes the relationship with its chosen vendor to be based upon the premise that *payment be made after successful performance by the vendor.* It is expected that the vendor and the company will draft a detailed set of systems and programming specifications together. In the event that it is not possible mutually to agree upon these specifications, the relationship will then terminate. Once these specifications have been established, future performance will be judged according to these specifications and according to a mutually agreed upon timetable. Checkpoints for performance judgment will be built into these specifications and payment terms tied to them. In no case can the company be obligated to accept delivery of hardware in advance of having been shown satisfactory system and software performance.

General Hardware Requirements

In this section, the general requirements for the hardware are given component by component. Note that the sample specifies which kinds of components should be present, or possible to attach later, and lets the vendor propose the number and sizes of these devices for the configuration. If the company is not sure which components should be present in the configuration, it is perfectly acceptable to ask each vendor to make a recommendation.

Sample

The system must include the following components:

1. Data entry devices: CRTs are desired. Punched cards or paper tape input cannot be considered.
2. Disk storage: must be sufficient to support the applications and functions described in this specification; must be modular and expandable enough to accommodate future growth.
3. Printer(s): must be reliable as this installation will not be able to tolerate downtime. It is anticipated that there will be a future need for uppercase and lowercase quality printing in a word processing application.
4. Tape drive: must be industry-compatible and reliable.
5. Central processing unit: must be sufficient to operate all of the system's devices in a responsive manner. The company prefers an on-line interactive system that updates transactions immediately upon entry and makes those transactions available to all other elements of the system. Response times averaging over five seconds on major applications are unacceptable.
6. Communications: the ability to access the system through a remote CRT over telephone lines is desirable in the future.

General Software Requirements

This area addresses the company's requirements with respect to basic software issues. Will the company accept packaged software or is customized software alone acceptable? Is there a minimum warranty period? To whom will the software belong after implementation? Must the software be written in a particular computer language? What constitutes adequate documentation? Again, mentioning these issues at the RFP stage paves the way for later discussions and can prevent unpleasant surprises down the road.

Sample

1. All applications software must be tailored to the applications requirements given in this document. Packages will be considered if they meet the company's requirements or may easily be modified to do so.
2. The software must be guaranteed by the vendor for at least a year after successful implementation by the vendor. Provision must be made for the swift resolution of any problems that may occur so that the company is not dependent upon the goodwill of the vendor to carry out its normal business functions.
3. The software, once completed, must become the property of the company. The company will agree not to sell the software so as to compete with the vendor.
4. The software must be fully documented so that the user has the resources to understand the physical and logical processes being performed by the system. "Fully documented" means including system and program narratives, system and program flowcharts, file and record layouts, and instructions for both entry and system level operators.
5. A higher level (compiler level) language must be available, or in its place a generalized report generator, so that the company has the ability to draw additional reports and analyses from its data base without being forced to seek assistance from a single source vendor. The company will agree not to modify elements of the system covered by the software warranty but needs the ability to draw from its own data on an ad hoc basis.

General System Functions Requirements

In this section, functions that the system must be able to perform, aside from the individual applications, are covered such as the periodic backing up of data and programs and the use of alternate hardware in the event of protracted down time. The sample also mentions upgrading expenditures and degradation.

Sample

1. The system must be designed to protect the company from the loss of data or the loss of ability to process. There must be provision for the regular creation and retention of backup files.
2. In case of hardware problems that cannot immediately be resolved, the company will need the ability to run its operations on another conveniently located system until the hardware problem is corrected.
3. The system must be upgradable and expandable without costly reprogramming or hardware expenditures above and beyond the cost of enlarging certain components.
4. There must not be degradation or contention among the elements of the system, which would prevent the hardware from accomplishing its expected volumes. In particular, the printing function must not preclude use of normal entry functions. Program development should be able to occur simultaneously with production activities.

Company Background

A description of the company's background and current business is tremendously helpful to a potential vendor in preparing a good proposal. Every business in the world has its own unique style, products, customers, and attitudes about what it does. An effective computer system needs to mesh with the unique aspects of the company it serves and cannot be at odds with the needs and feelings of its management.

This section can describe how the company was founded and its course of development to the present. It may cover how its products are developed, produced, marketed, and sold. Finally, it should indicate management's judgments of what is important in running the business.

Sample

Company Background

The Gooseneck Lamp Co. was founded in 1926 by Mr. J. Robert Jones, whose patented flexible tube was the forerunner of the now world famous gooseneck lamp. The current president, Bob Jones, is the grandson of the founder.

Since 1926 the company has grown to its present level of one hundred employees. Gooseneck lamps are unique for their ability to be adjusted to provide good working light in any direction.

The company maintains a plant in the Cleveland area. The plant produces an average of one thousand lamps per day, in six different styles and twelve different colors.

Gooseneck lamps are sold wholesale to department stores and bookstores; the average order is for fifty lamps. They are also sold wholesale to thirty mail-order catalog companies. The company operates a retail store in a Cleveland suburb, where discontinued styles and factory seconds are sold at a discount. The company employs eight salesmen in total.

The company has developed a high-intensity pocket gooseneck flashlight, ideal for use by doctors and nurses, which it wishes to market to the medical profession. It plans to develop an intensive marketing campaign to promote this new product in the medical marketplace.

All of the company's systems and procedures are currently manual, with the exception of the payroll, which is processed at a local payroll service bureau.

Management is concerned about its ability to support the marketing thrust of the new flashlight without a computer system to assist. A computer is regarded as essential to monitor the sales of the new product, so that the company can take advantage of marketing successes where they occur and not dilute its limited efforts in markets that do not work out well. If the campaign is successful, management feels that existing clerical order fulfillment procedures will be inadequate to handle the increased volume of business without having an unsatisfactory effect on customer service, of which the company is very proud.

Applications

Each application should have been investigated thoroughly in the process of preparing the RFP. The applications sections constitute the heart of the RFP.

For each application, several subjects should be covered in fair detail.

First, the purpose of the application as far as the company is concerned should be addressed. This may sound like a dull, unnecessary task. However you may find unusual answers when you really pursue the question of purpose with respect to each application. What is the true purpose of sending out customer statements? What would happen if you didn't?

Second, what is now being done should be described in simple terms. It is important to make this section specific but brief so that the reader can get an overview of the processing involved.

Third, make mention of the changes you would like to see. Try to separate those about which you are adamant, the musts, from those that mean less to you. Mention desired improvements whether or not you think the computer could bring them about.

If you have the help of someone versed in systems analysis and/or computerized business systems, you may be able to go further and design your own ideal system. In this case you may be able to specify some requirements for your new system in the fourth section. If you are without technical help, you may want to consider hiring a consultant (see Chapter 11). Without help, the best you can do is lay out the improvements you would like to make and challenge the vendors to design a system that meets your needs. In either case, Chapter 10 reviews useful features that may be included to advantage in typical business data processing applications.

The sample application given here is that of accounts receivable, an application that all companies have in some form and which most find cost-effective to computerize.

In the sample, it is first assumed that the company has no access to a consultant or analyst familiar with business data processing systems. The sample lists the desired improvements without making reference to systematized solutions. The list is straightforward and should enable an experienced vendor to identify and implement a successful accounts receivable application.

A requirements section is then appended that might have been prepared by a consultant or analyst familiar with computerized business systems. The problems listed in the Desired Improvements section are addressed with specific solutions, which are expressed as requirements. Even an inexperienced vendor, were he to meet the requirements as listed, could implement a successful system.

Sample

F. *Accounts Receivable*

1. *Purpose.* The company wishes its accounts receivable application to fulfill three purposes:

a. To provide service to customers by providing charge facilities
b. To enable management to know the amount owed by customers at any time
c. To facilitate collection efforts as much as possible

2. *Existing procedures.* A ledger card exists for each customer and is filed in a tub file. As invoices are prepared, the A/R clerk posts them to the appropriate customer's ledger card and brings the new customer balance forward. As cash is received, it is posted to a new line on the customer's ledger card and a reduced balance is brought forward. At the end of the month, the clerk manually prepares an aged trial balance, spreading the customer's unpaid balance into appropriate aging columns and totaling the columns. This effort takes three working days. Customer statements, prepared after the aged trial balance, consist of a single figure, the unpaid balance. Statements are hand typed, taking three working days to prepare. The aged trial balance is used for the identification of delinquent customers, who are sent a succession of form letters of increasingly serious tone. General ledger entries are manually prepared from the aged trial balance and manual additions of cash receipts and invoice transactions.

3. *Desired improvements.*

a. Simplify the preparation of the aged trial balance and customer statements. They take three days each. No invoices or cash can be applied until they are finished.
b. Show more detail on customer statements. Many customers question the single figure as they do not know which invoices and payments have been included.
c. Simplify the process of posting invoices. Because of clerical workloads, they are frequently posted late. An enormous catch-up effort is required at month's end, or the statements go out late.
d. Be able to link cash payments with particular invoices.
e. Make it easier to know an account's up-to-date status and balance.

f. Have some way to prevent customers with seriously overdue balances from placing further orders.

The information above amply illustrates the problems being experienced with the present manual accounts receivable system. To have written this information, all that should have been required was a good set of eyes and ears! An experienced vendor should be able to convert this list of problems into a set of solutions.

Had the company in the sample used a consultant or analyst, the following requirements might have been added to the applications writeup.

Sample (continued)

4. *Requirements for computerization.*

a. The company requires a true open item system. Each invoice transaction remains on file until fully resolved by payment, adjustment, or some combination of payments and adjustments, amounting to the full amount of the original invoice.

b. Cash receipts need to be applied directly to the invoice to which they pertain. If the cash receipt cannot be associated with a particular invoice, it is applied "on account" and constitutes a separate open item with a credit balance. A cash receipts register follows the termination of the cash receipts function and lists and totals all of the cash receipts transactions.

c. An aged trial balance will be produced by the system. Sorted by customer, it will contain full detail about all of the open items present for that customer, showing the customer's balance broken down by aging category. The name and address of the customer as given in the customer master file will be printed as well. Totals at the end of the report will summarize all receivables for the company by aging category.

d. The open items will be purged monthly. The purge will remove open items that have a zero balance and have been fully resolved by payment and/or adjustment. The purge is run after the aged trial balance, which will have printed the purged items for one final time before they leave the system as an audit trail. The purge is run before the customer statements, which means that they will show only open items going into the new month, not open items that have been paid and resolved.

e. Invoices will be posted automatically to accounts receivable after they have been printed. An invoice register will accompany the posting process and will list and total all of the transactions added to the accounts receivable file.
f. An inquiry facility will exist whereby a customer's balance and open items can be reviewed. The inquiry process should be made available to all users, regardless of their security password.
g. A delinquency report shall be made available to the person in charge of collections. It will list customers who are considered delinquent, based upon some definition of number of days and dollars overdue. The report may be in the same format as the aged trial balance. The person in charge of collections may decide to refuse to extend credit to seriously delinquent accounts.
h. Persons to whom credit is no longer extended are coded "stop credit" in the customer master file. The order entry programs will not allow completion of an order for a customer with a stop credit code.

System Files, Transaction Counts, and Statistics

If this data has not been included in the individual applications sections, it can be assembled here. This section is a table showing numbers of entities and transactions, both at the present time and in the future. To give expected future data, estimate what the volumes will be in a three-year period and then double the figure. Remember, you are not committing to buy adequate hardware to meet these volumes now, but you would like to guarantee that it *will be possible* to buy that much hardware in the future.

Sample

System Files, Transaction Counts, and Statistics

	Current Volumes	Growth Requirements
Customer accounts	500	2000
Accounts receivable open items	2000	6000
Orders per month	400	1000
Inventory items	30	60
Accounts payable vendors	200	400
Accounts payable open items	500	1000
General ledger accounts	200	300
Invoices per month	400	1000
Cash receipts per month	300	600

CHAPTER TEN

Elements of Successful Applications Design

We would all agree that there are a number of ways to do almost anything; hence the saying, "There are lots of ways to skin a cat." And generally, some ways work better than others; hence another saying, "If at first you don't succeed, try, try again." Your minicomputer system is not the place to experiment with system designs. You would rather do it right the first time and use the energy that redoing it would require for something more constructive.

This chapter will describe elements of minicomputer applications design that have worked well. Some of the elements fit all applications; others, specific applications. The specific applications design techniques, however, will work on many systems.

Give the Operator a Lot of Guidance

Make every communication from the system to the operator clear and concise. Present the operator with the possible responses to any question being asked. For example, "Do you have any more entries (Y/N)?" is a straightforward question that provides the operator with the possible responses. In a more complicated question with a more difficult required response, such as "Enter the customer's category (2 digits or H)," the operator has the opportunity to key the letter H to ask for help. When H is keyed, the program can display a list of rules for assigning customer categories and then return to the question, asking for a two-digit category number.

These are merely samples of the kind of operator assistance

that can be planned into the system. For every response from the operator, concern should be addressed to the very real possibility that the operator will not know how to respond; hence, as much assistance should be built into the process as possible. Attention to this aspect of system operations will have a number of far-reaching benefits. First, it will enable relatively untrained personnel to operate the system from its (and their) first day, which in the long run will save personnel dollars. Second, it will lessen operator dependence upon instruction books and documentation, which should still exist but will not be in constant use. This will save considerable time over the life of the system, another economic benefit. Third, better data will go into the system and therefore will come out of the system, which makes the system more useful, accurate, dependable, and reliable to all its users. Giving as much assistance as possible to the operators of the system will pay off handsomely, and should be a primary consideration in the design of every program, function, screen format, and system request.

Take Advantage of Menu Techniques

Menus embody the concept of giving maximum assistance to the operator. Just as they do in a restaurant, computer menus present a clear list of alternatives to be chosen from. Generally menus are used to move from one application to another and from one program or function to another within an application. The following menu might be presented to an operator who had just "signed on" to the system.

```
GOOSENECK LAMP COMPANY
      MAIN MENU


1. CUSTOMER MENU
2. ORDER ENTRY MENU
3. INVOICING MENU
4. ACCOUNTS RECEIVABLE MENU
5. ACCOUNTS PAYABLE MENU
6. GENERAL LEDGER MENU
7. INVENTORY MENU


99. EXIT THIS MENU

    ENTER CHOICE :
```

Let us assume that the operator entered 1, choosing the customer menu. The next menu displayed on the screen might look like this:

```
GOOSENECK LAMP COMPANY
    CUSTOMER MENU


 1. ADD A NEW CUSTOMER
 2. CHANGE AN EXISTING CUSTOMER
 3. INQUIRE ON A CUSTOMER
 4. PRINT ALPHABETICAL CUSTOMER LISTING
 5. PRINT CUSTOMERS BY ZIP CODE
 6. CUSTOMER PURGE PROCEDURE


99. EXIT THIS MENU

    ENTER CHOICE :
```

The operator could choose any of the functions or reports listed above. The operator could also return to the main menu by keying 99. Note here that the operator does not need to remember names of programs or procedures to operate these functions but is just asked to make straightforward choices of clear alternatives.

Limit Menu Access for Security Purposes

You might feel that your ordinary order entry operator would have no need to access the accounts payable, general ledger, or other functions. This is commonly true. With the menu approach, it is relatively simple to accomplish such security objectives.

When operators sign on to the system, the system should ask them to identify themselves with a password or other code. The password or other identification is assigned to each operator by the system manager and indicates to the system what access is granted to its user. It is a simple matter of programming to alter the contents of each menu displayed to an operator to reflect his access privileges.

For example, here is the main menu modified to reflect the access privileges of the ordinary order entry operator, who (it has been decided by the company) is not expected to perform general ledger, accounts payable, inventory, or accounts receivable functions:

```
GOOSENECK LAMP COMPANY
       MAIN MENU


 1. CUSTOMER MENU
 2. ORDER ENTRY MENU
 3. INVOICING MENU


99. EXIT THIS MENU

    ENTER CHOICE :
```

Even within the applications to which this operator has been given access, there may be functions that management does not wish performed. Here is the customer menu limited by the privilege level of this operator:

```
     GOOSENECK LAMP COMPANY
         CUSTOMER MENU


     1. ADD A NEW CUSTOMER
     2. CHANGE AN EXISTING CUSTOMER
     3. INQUIRE ON A CUSTOMER
     4. PRINT ALPHABETICAL CUSTOMER LISTING
     5. PRINT CUSTOMERS BY ZIP CODE


    99. EXIT THIS MENU

         ENTER CHOICE :
```

In this example, management has decided that operators at this level should not be initiating the customer purge procedure. Another way of accomplishing the same goal might be to begin the customer purge procedure with a request for a password or other indication of authorization. In this way the purge procedure could stay on the menu but could not be run by an unauthorized person. The word "unauthorized" here means untrained rather than untrustworthy. Generally, more damage is done to systems by well-meaning people making mistakes than by those with bad intentions. It is important that the system designers protect the system from both kinds of people!

Note that by using this approach of limiting access to parts of the system through menu modifications, the programs themselves are not involved. As new employees are trained to operate the system and old ones leave, passwords and security identification codes may be changed constantly though the programs themselves require no changes. A menu-based security arrangement is easy to set up and to maintain.

Acknowledge the Need to Inquire

It is good for several reasons to encourage users of the system to make inquiries of it. You eliminate the need for large reference reports. Users of traditional batch and mainframe systems have no choice but to print mammoth listings of their data so that questions can be answered. Not only is the information in these reports out-of-date after some point, but the time and expense spent printing the number of copies necessary can be considerable. Even worse, whole files are usually printed out, as the precise nature of the questions to be asked cannot be known in advance. By allowing users access to inquiry functions through a terminal, they can reference just the information they need—and the information will be as up-to-date as the system can have it.

As a general principle, it is smart to permit inquiries to the system in every area where inquiries can be productive. Some logical questions that inquiry functions can easily answer are listed here:

—What is the complete name and address on file for a particular customer?
—What open receivable items does a particular customer have right now?
—How much of a particular inventory item is now in stock?
—What orders does a particular customer have with us now?
—What orders are open for a particular inventory item?
—How much do we owe a particular vendor?
—Is a particular vendor invoice paid yet?
—What is the balance of a particular general ledger account?
—What were the transactions against a certain general ledger account last month?

Some individuals may not need to know about certain areas of the system; as we have seen, their access may be restricted by a security password. Those who do have the right and need to know may lack proper training to perform particular operations. Such people, often in top management positions, may be given security privileges that allow them to inquire into all areas of the system. Note that the system is protected from their lack of training as they cannot possibly make an error that affects the system while only inquiring.

Provide for Regular File Purges

Today's minicomputer systems are usually designed to have all their data resident and available at all times. In traditional mainframe systems, however, data was loaded into the machine for the time of processing and then removed.

The question of purging minicomputer files is a very important one given the fact that disk storage is limited even if purchased in very large quantities. If no provision is made for removing deadwood from a system, its demands for storage will constantly grow and its processing speed will be slowed by the necessity of bypassing useless data. Some users decide to purchase enough storage to contain everything for a long time and to live with the lessened efficiency of processing. This decision, however, ought to be made with full appreciation of the trade-offs involved. Indeed, most users make some provision to purge their files as a regular part of processing.

How do you know what to purge and when? Each file on the system needs to be analyzed on its own merits. The pattern of data flow into the file, its expected growth, and the ways in which data outlives its usefulness must be considered. In general, master files such as the customer file, inventory file, and general ledger account files are more difficult to purge than files that contain transactions, which are more short-lived.

Accounts receivable transactions that have been paid or otherwise resolved can usually leave the system in the month following their resolution. Usually it is a good idea to include these transactions on the month-end aged trial balance as an audit trail. Then, if questions occur, the data exists in printed form, if no longer in the system. The same principle holds true for the accounts payable transactions representing paid vendor invoices. They, too, can be printed on one final aged trial balance at month-end and removed from the system. These files can then be sized to contain the average number of open items, plus the maximum number of resolved items that can occur in a month, along with sufficient space to grow.

Orders that have been invoiced, picked, packed, and shipped can be removed from the system once the logical period for customer questions has expired. Ideally any sales history data will have been posted from them before they are removed.

General ledger transactions for a given month may be posted to the master accounts involved in total at month-end. They may also be listed on the general ledger trial balance, which shows for each account its opening balance, transactions for the month, and closing balance.

The customer master file needs special analysis to determine what and when to purge. It is a basic accounting concept that customers with receivables (either debit or credit balances!) should not be removed from the system. Beyond that consideration, it certainly would not make sense to remove a customer with an open or back order. Different companies have different ways of determining at what point in time a customer becomes inactive and should be dropped, if ever. The considerations involve the normal buying patterns of customers, the nature of the product being sold (some products depend on repeat business), and other factors.

On one system it was decided that customers who had not made a purchase or a payment during the preceding six months should be purged. Each customer's master record contained several fields that the system kept up-to-date. The invoicing process posted the "date of last invoice" field when the customer was invoiced, and the cash receipts process posted the "date of last payment" field when cash was applied to the customer. The system linked orders and receivables to the customer and could detect when neither was present. The company decided not to discard totally the names and addresses of these inactive customers but to write them off onto a reel of magnetic tape, which is cheap to store and could be used to bring the names back into the system easily. Finally, the company acknowledged that the people operating the system might be aware of extenuating circumstances vis-à-vis a customer's ostensible inactivity and thus printed the names of customers about to be dropped prior to the purge; management reviewed the lists and was able to veto the dropping of any customer.

During the analysis of each area of the system and how to purge it, the value of having the ability to use magnetic tape on a system becomes apparent. As the preceding example demonstrates, it is far easier to commit to removing data if it is stored elsewhere for possible reuse. Magnetic tape is cheap and easy to store, and can be extremely useful in retaining data that will be of later use but is currently in the way! An example of retaining data in this way is the customer purge mentioned above. The names purged from the customer file were retained on tape, and used once a year for promotional mailing purposes. Another example would be the retention of general ledger transactions purged each month until year end, when a yearly analysis of expenses and summary trial balance could be created.

Don't Give the System Too Much Authority

As you no doubt noted in the customer purge example given above, human intervention was planned into the process. By allowing management to review the list of customers about to be purged from the system, the system's planners built in flexibility. First, they acknowledged that their view of the way the purge process might work might not hold up over time. Often the planning process takes place months or years before the system is implemented and by that time many aspects of the business may have changed. Second, they acknowledged that there might be errors in the implementation of the process, such as program bugs or misunderstanding of how the entire procedure should take place. Human reviewers could identify customers who should not be purged, which the computer might not be able to. Third, they acknowledged that the system would never have certain information that the people operating it might have, such as knowledge of extenuating circumstances.

It is always wise to plan a safety valve before the system takes a serious and perhaps irreversible step. It is far easier to repair a problem that *almost* occurred than one that has already done its damage. If in the future the safety valve turns out not to be useful, it can be removed.

Make Functions Modular

Don't construct any one process to be totally performed by just one program that does many jobs. Rather, link a number of programs, each of which does its own small jobs, together to execute one after the other. With smaller, modular processes, it is easier to make modifications, to detect and repair problems, and to recover in case of trouble. For example, the customer purge discussed above could consist of the following separate steps:

1. Erase all existing tags on customers.
2. Tag all customers with open orders or back orders.
3. Tag all customers with open receivables.
4. Tag customers with invoicing or payments within the last six months.

5. Select all untagged customers.
6. List untagged customers on the printer.
7. Invite the operator to tag any customers who ought not to be deleted.
8. Record untagged customers onto tape.
9. Delete untagged customers from the system.

Systems that do not invite user participation in serious procedures tend to take on a relentless and unyielding aspect in the minds of their users. It is far better to plan a system that behaves "politely" with its users' data.

Provide Restart Procedures Everywhere

A system's strength rests not only on the elegance of the functions it performs but also on the solidarity and reliability of its performance. Murphy's law governs the mysterious inner workings of hardware, and people are not infallible either. Whatever the cause for malfunctions, they will occur; accordingly, it is a good idea to design restart capabilities for every system function. The instructions for running every job should include instructions for restarting in the event that it is necessary.

Take a simple job like listing customer names and addresses. Suppose customers are listed alphabetically and the printer jams in the midst of the letter P, destroying two full pages after having printed two hundred good pages. Is the entire job to be started over again? It certainly would be far more efficient to resume printing at the point where the printer jammed. The ability to do this is one of the differences between okay and wonderful systems and is quite simple to provide.

Part of restarting a job is knowing where it died. On a printed report this point may be obvious. On a function that sorts or updates files, it may not be so easy to identify the place where processing was interrupted. One of the traditionally successful methods of informing the world about the progress of a job is to display something meaningful on the screen as the system functions; the meaningful thing may be the customer's account number or name or other field that will indicate the progress the function has made so far. Displaying such a progress indicator on the screen has other benefits. Although it may seem silly, many functions are aborted by operators who become convinced that the job has died or gotten stuck. Operators of systems get very nervous when a process goes for a long time and does not "do" anything. Thus, it is wise to provide the reassurance that a display of progress will give; it is considerate as well, for the operator can extrapolate from the progress made and predict the rough ending point of the job most of the time. (Knowing when a job is likely to end can be of great assistance in planning the work flow of a system, thereby improving efficiency.)

Avoid Looking Up Codes

Traditional batch and mainframe systems have required that the identities involved in most transactions be submitted in coded form. For example, in the typical accounts payable system, a vendor invoice transaction has to carry the correct code of the vendor involved and usually a number of other codes, too. When the transaction enters the system, it is compared against the vendor master file. If the code does not match a code there, a message prints out on the error listing created by the editing procedure. The transaction is recoded and resubmitted for processing. Even if the code matches one in the vendor master file, there is no guarantee that the code belongs to the intended vendor. We have discussed these limitations of batch and mainframe systems in reviewing the advantages afforded by interactive processing. In this example, it would work very differently with an interactive system. The operator would enter the vendor's code (leaving aside for the moment where the code comes from) and the program controlling the entry would look for that code in the vendor master file. If the code were not present there, the system would so inform the operator and ask for another code. If the code were there, the system would display the name and address of the vendor to whom that code belonged and ask for verification by the operator that this vendor was indeed the correct vendor. If the operator, on inspecting the name and address, noted that it was not the correct vendor, a negative reply would be given and the process would be repeated. With this procedure, the operator verifies visually the vendor being used for the transaction and avoids the cumbersome edit–list errors–make corrections–resubmit transaction cycle.

But where does the vendor's code come from? With batch and mainframe systems, the vendor's code is typically a numeric code; the assigned number usually represents the approximate alphabetical position of that vendor among all vendors. Numeric codes are used by designers of batch and mainframe systems to provide an alphabetic sequence while avoiding a time-consuming sort of twenty or twenty-five alphabetic characters. Numeric codes do save time sorting but cannot be remembered or surmised at all. Typcially, stacks of transactions (vendor invoices for our example) are sent through a coding process whereby clerks look up the codes in large printouts of master records. Once the vendor is located, his code is written on the transaction document, which usually next goes through the keypunch process. Note here that the coding process depends on having up-to-date printouts to work with and is vulnerable to transcription errors.

With an interactive system, we can almost totally avoid this looking up process. First, the operator is sitting at a terminal and is connected to data more up-to-date than any printed listing can ever be. Second, more trial and error can be allowed in the interactive process, as the vendor's name and address will be displayed on the screen for verification. That is, there are more possible ways of finding the vendor as it will be quite obvious whether a given way has been successful. The remaining problem is to structure an appropriate starting entry by the operator to begin the looking up process within the system itself. Ideally, the operator's entry comes directly from the document at hand. Today, the overwhelming majority of businesses include their name, address, and zip code on all their documents. A vendor code that contains the vendor's zip code and some alphabetic characters from the vendor's name can be used to attempt to locate the vendor within the vendor master file. The system will respond with the name and address of any vendor on file with that "alpha-zip." If the displayed vendor is not the desired one, the system can continue displaying names and addresses of vendors with matching alpha-zips until there are no more. Other alpha-zips can be tried if the first was not successful.

The advantages to a system that employs such a scheme are tremendous. Note that no prior coding step takes place with the document being entered. The operator uses information already on the document (vendor name and address, including zip code) to construct or surmise a trial code. The system cooperates by displaying all the possibilities for that trial code until the desired vendor is located. No large printouts are created and the operator does not have to get up to obtain anything. Even if three or four different codes are tried through the system, the process is still faster than the manual route that would have to be followed instead. And with the visual display of the chosen vendor, the error level drops.

The success of such a "self-coded" procedure obviously depends upon the nature of the structure chosen. With files that consist mainly of names and addresses in the United States, this alpha-zip approach works well; few entries exist under the same alpha-zip. (Customers or vendors starting with "National," "American," etc., in large metropolitan areas within the same zip code are usually the duplicates. Most other names separate nicely by zip code.) Experiment with an alpha-zip structure for customer and vendor files under twenty thousand names.

In other situations, good system design can create multiple ways to find a given record in the system. Partial name searches can be utilized. If the document being entered into the system is one that the system itself produced at some prior time (typically a customer invoice that is now being paid), information already in the system can be used to great advantage as an entry code. For example, for payment of a customer's invoice, enter only the invoice number (which by definition is unique and on file as a receivable) and let the system look up the identity of the customer in the invoice on file!

During the systems analysis process, each transaction should be scrutinized in an attempt to identify information in it that can be used to enter the transaction into the system in the most efficient way. Programs should then be structured to work with information already on the document or existing within the system to aid in processing the transaction. Countless hours of effort can be saved by attention to the coding processes involved.

Make Functions Operate in Reverse

This concept is important for two reasons. First, people frequently make mistakes. They make more when learning a new thing but will inevitably make some even when fully trained. Thus, it is crucial to make a system forgiving, able easily to cancel the effects of an error. Obviously, there is a point in every process at which it is too late to undo a mistake. But until that point, it should be as easy as possible either to cancel everything and start over or to correct a minor error. For example, in order entry, it should be possible to modify or cancel an order up until the time when the invoice or picking slip is printed. After that point, a more formal adjustment or cancellation procedure should be used. The premise here is that it is much easier to modify or cancel an order before it is printed than to issue a credit memo later!

The second reason that being able to operate in reverse is important is that often the reverse of a normal transaction is a very useful function in itself. Take, for example, a typical cash receipts transaction. The transaction normally consists of a positive amount of cash applied to reduce a receivable. But could the reverse, a negative amount of cash, be used to increase a receivable? Yes, it is a very useful technique. First, allowing the reverse of the normal transaction makes it simple to correct and offset keying errors immediately by using the same program functions. Second, the technique allows the operator in effect to move a cash payment from one open item to another within a customer account through the cash receipts procedure. Say, for example, that a certain payment was applied to the wrong invoice of a customer. By paying the right invoice of that customer and unpaying the wrong one, the net cash effect is zero; this correction can be accomplished through normal cash receipts processing in a very simple way. The same principle holds true in accounts payable, where a negative vendor invoice transaction represents a return or a chargeback.

Take Advantage of Table Techniques

A simple technique that greatly enhances a system is the widespread use of tables. Tables can be thought of as *lists* in which the system can look up things. A common kind of table is a "tax table," which lists all of the tax jurisdictions where sales tax is to be charged and gives the effective tax rate for each. Another kind of table can link postal zip codes to UPS zone codes.

Tables do change over time (for example, a city may change its sales tax rate) but do not change with great frequency. However, since the information is expected to change at some point, it is wise not to build the information itself into the programs that need it, as then the programs themselves will have to be changed every time the information is changed. Instead, it is smarter to have the program structured to access a table to get the information it needs. The contents of the table should be under the control of the system's users, who are then responsible for keeping the table accurate and up-to-date. When information changes, the user changes the table; the programmer does not have to change the program. The user of course should be provided with a convenient and easy way to keep the table in good shape. Generally, there is a program that offers the user the opportunity to add entries, delete entries, and modify existing entries in table. Tables can be used for standard invoice messages, discount rates, tax rates, salesperson commissions, and many other small collections of information.

The above design concepts pertain to all applications. Next we will investigate concepts that apply to certain applications but are not unique to any particular company's requirements. The unique requirements of a particular company's applications obviously cannot be discussed here, but some of the concepts mentioned can be transferred in theory to any company's system design.

Customer File Design

As mentioned above, a lot of consideration should be given to the plan for purging the customer file. Obviously, the customer should not have any receivables, orders, or back orders pending. Moreover, some thought should be given to the process of determining whether a customer is no longer active. For each business, the process may be a different one, and the data carried in the customer file should include all facts necessary to make that process work. Some businesspeople may wonder why they shouldn't leave *all* customers on file. That, too, is an acceptable alternative provided that analysis has determined how many customers there are and what growth will occur over time and management is willing to commit enough disk storage and processing time to leave them in the system.

Attention also needs to be given to the subject of making the customer easy to find in the system when entering a transaction against him. The alpha-zip coding scheme works effectively in identifying customers from their own documents. The documents being used to process transactions should be reviewed and all possible methods of accessing the parties involved should be investigated and analyzed. If necessary, several alternative access methods can be constructed to assist the operator.

Many facts about a customer rarely change and are used in the process of taking and filling orders. Some of these facts, for example, are UPS zone, tax code, preferred shipping method, and salesperson number. It makes a great deal of sense to set these facts up in the customer master file, as they do change infrequently. When the customer is identified during the order entry process, the facts can be drawn from the customer master file. The operator may be allowed to override these facts if they do not apply to the order at hand. But much of the time they will apply, and drawing them from the customer file will save time.

Order Entry and Invoicing Design

As mentioned above, make the customer easy to find in the system by using the order document itself and thereby avoiding a prior coding step. Pick up constant information about the customer from the customer master file instead of keying these facts for every order. Allow the operator to override this constant information if it does not apply to a particular order.

A sequential order number works well. Normally the system assigns this number by adding one to a counter. The number stays with the order for the life of the order. As the system assigns the next sequential number, the number is noted by the operator from the screen and written on the actual order document. Ideally, the system's inquiry functions help the user learn the number of a particular order once he has identified the customer or given other identifying facts about the order. Thus, the order number, since the system can provide it if it is not known, can be an effective filing number. Customer order documents and other relevant paperwork can be conveniently filed by this number, which is basically a chronologically sequenced number. Companies that had been filing numerous copies of orders and invoices in several ways (for example, one by customer, another by invoice number, and a third by salesperson) have found that they need only one set of files, arranged by sequential order number, and that the system can cross-reference to that number given any of the other numbers. This concept of a single set of files with the system providing cross-references to it ties in with the concept of building versatile inquiry capabilities into the system through multiple access methods. The three concepts, when implemented in an integrated way, can dramatically simplify a company's filing, recordkeeping, and researching functions at great savings.

Consider also the possibility of entering a customer's prepayment of an order directly into the order entry process. Companies whose customers do a high volume of prepayment or credit card payment find that customers appreciate having the prepayment shown on the invoice or shipping document. Confirming receipt of prepayment can also prevent customer questions. The prepayment recorded at order entry time can be posted directly to accounts receivable along with the invoice amount, so no additional keying is necessary to record the prepayment during order entry.

Consider using a "tickler system" in conjunction with order entry. A tickler system, which is easy to program, makes a simple note in the system that some event is supposed to happen on or before a certain date. The event can be the shipment of an order or back order or a telephone call. Orders that pass their due date without having the event occur are listed for management review. These listings serve as excellent reminders of things that are behind schedule. Staff members will come to appreciate and depend on a tickler system that is tied to an order entry system.

In many instances a message (or messages) should appear on a customer's invoice or packing slip. Messages may explain out-of-stock conditions, substitutions, or back orders, or they may announce special sale items. Often the same message text is applicable to numerous situations. Tables of standard messages can be set up and the messages summoned by brief mnemonic codes, which saves keying time. As with all such tables, the contents of the standard messages should be under user control.

An invoice register should always be printed for the group of invoices just printed. Each invoice is recapped by a one-line entry on the register, showing bill-to, ship-to, invoice number, date, and dollar amounts for merchandise, tax, shipping, prepayment, and total invoice amount. At the end of the listing totals are given for each of the dollar fields. In addition, breakdowns of the total tax charged by taxing jurisdiction should be shown, along with any other information that might be necessary for general ledger postings. If a general ledger system has been implemented, the postings can be made either directly at this time or manually from the listing, which is an audit trail.

Inventory File Design

The inventory file is another place where coding schemes can be structured to make it easier to locate products in the system. The inventory file can contain products or services. Included normally are the description of the product, its price, and the quantities on hand, allocated to existing orders, and on reorder from vendors.

Most staff members who work with inventory are familiar with the "part numbers" or names of many different products. If such a memory base already exists, it may make sense to keep the existing item number structure in the new system. If, on the other hand, the inventory file is expected to have a great many items in it and/or the present coding scheme is not easy to remember, you may want to utilize a self-coding scheme such as the ones suggested previously. Key words from the name of the item can form an access method. Ideally, the method would fit into the terminology that customers use when ordering the item.

The proper access method for the inventory file very much depends upon the specific situation. Inventory file design, more than any other area of a system, is subject to the precise requirements of the company involved. One method that has worked well in a number of applications is the "generic code." With this technique, all items in the inventory are classified as being in one or another category of product on a generic basis. The categories are given easily remembered mnemonic abbreviations. An inquirer into the system can specify the generic category in which he is interested and the system will display descriptions of the various inventory items contained in that category, along with their item numbers. The inquirer (or order entry operator) can then select the item he wants and use its item number to continue the inquiry. This is an example of using multiple access methods simultaneously.

Most inventory systems need some control over stock levels. The inventory record for each item can indicate the desired maximum and minimum stock levels for that item. The levels can be different for each item, as they will logically have different reorder and replenishment schedules and requirements. If helpful, maximums and minimums can be developed by the system. The system can keep track of a rolling average monthly sales level for a specified number of months. Management can then enter into each item's record the maximum and minimum number of average months' sales as stock levels it wishes to stay between. Thus, if sales increase, the calculated maximum and minimum on-hand quantities will also increase without any intervention. Items that are either under or over their acceptable range of stock levels will be printed out on an exception listing periodically. Management can review these listings and make adjustments in the reorder or restocking process for the item.

Accounts Receivable

Use the same techniques to locate the customer as have been previously discussed, allowing the operator to search the system files with information available directly from the document being processed. A common transaction is the payment of cash for the invoices produced by the system. Often customers provide a copy of the invoice being paid, if one is provided and requested to be returned, or they will reference the invoice number(s) on their payment check. Using the invoice number to access the customer is a timesaving technique.

Occasionally a payment will be received for an unknown invoice from a known customer. In that case, the system needs a convenient way to place the payment on account for that customer, effectively creating a new open item with a credit balance in the process. Also, payments will be received for unknown invoices and unknown customers. These payments generally involve a fair amount of detective work to track down the identity of the payer. A simple program can list all of the open receivables of the same dollar amount as the payment and immensely facilitate the effort of determining whose account to apply the check to.

Order entry programs can assist credit and collection efforts by applying credit limits to orders when they are entered. The customer file can contain a field giving the maximum credit that has been allowed for each customer. Order entry can check that the current receivables plus the order being entered do not exceed the limit and notify the operator if supervisory action is necessary. Order entry can also be prevented if the customer has been placed on credit hold by the collections department, in which case the system will not allow orders to be keyed in against that customer. Flexible grading of customers can be accomplished by having the month-end aged trial balance program assess the customer's current receivables standing and assign an appropriate grade to each customer. This grade will change when the customer's standing changes and will automatically prohibit order entry if the standing reaches a predetermined point.

A display of current customer open items is a must in a good receivables system. There should be a display feature built into both the customer inquiry function and the cash receipts function so that the operator can identify the open items upon which it would be possible to apply a payment that is not specified as being against a particular invoice. The display should include for each open item its number, date, amount, perhaps the customer's purchase order number, and optionally the date and nature of any payments against the item. If the items present more than fill one screen, the ability to see more items should be provided.

The aged trial balance is printed at month-end. It shows the customer name and address, each open item and its amount and age, and aged totals for the customer. It shows totals at the end of the report for all customers, giving the total open items aged by date ranges (thirty, sixty, ninety days, etc.).

If the aged trial balance is run before the normal end-of-month purge of resolved receivables, it can provide a handy audit trail of the transactions that will subsequently leave the system.

Customer statements can be run before or after the purge, depending upon whether management wishes to show resolved receivables on the statement or not. Some users feel that the presence of resolved receivables is a distraction to customers and detracts from the purpose of the statement, which is to remind customers of open and unpaid items. Certainly, the printing of these resolved items on the statement takes more forms and more time. Other users feel that they can reduce the number of customer inquiries by showing resolved items on the statement. Neither way is right or wrong; it depends on your company's practices.

The cash receipts function should allow the reduction of open items to be balanced against postings to the general ledger rather than against actual cash. In this way, balances too small to be worth collecting can be written off immediately during the cash receipts process. An example might be several pennies of difference between the invoice amount and the cash payment. The pennies can be written off to a "pennies variance account" in the general ledger rather than carried as a receivable not likely to be collected. True write-offs of uncollectible items can also be accomplished with cash receipts, perhaps protected with a password so that unauthorized persons do not have access to the function. The cash receipts function should be followed with the printing of a cash receipts journal showing each of the transactions that occurred. Totals at the end of the journal should include the total change to accounts receivable, the total cash payments, and the recapped postings to the various general ledger accounts mentioned during the transaction session. These totals can be automatically posted to the general ledger, if implemented, or can be the source for manual general ledger postings.

Each month's aged trial balance should be balanced against the previous month's trial balance, by taking the previous receivables total, adding to it the new debits shown on all of the invoice registers for the month, and subtracting from it all of the credits to receivables shown on all of the cash receipts journals for the month. The new trial balance should balance to this total.

Accounts Payable

Techniques that make it easy to locate the vendor should be utilized, as previously discussed.

As vendor invoices are entered, the distribution of the invoice amount to the various general ledger expense accounts should be requested from the operator. As each general ledger account code is entered, the program should check that it does exist and is valid for posting. The amounts posted to all general ledger accounts should balance to the exact amount of the invoice before the process can terminate. Invoice entry should include a way to specify a vendor discount and to identify the time period for which the discount is valid. It should also be possible to specify that only part of the invoice amount is subject to the discount, as many vendors will not discount freight and other "pass-along" costs.

A strong inquiry feature should exist so that the user can identify the precise status of a vendor and his open items. If the screen fills, the opportunity should be given to see more.

There should be a handy way or variety of ways to select the items to be paid at a given time. The operator might be given the opportunity to make the selection by the due date of the items on file, so that all items due on or before a given date could be selected for payment. Selection by discount date or by vendor are other possibilities. The more flexibility, the better.

Once the items are selected, they can be printed on a "pre-check listing" for management review. Management can delete things it doesn't want paid at this time and add items that were not selected. When the pre-check listing is satisfactory, the actual checks should be run.

Make sure that the check printing process appropriately handles negative vendor balances. These can occur if the amounts of chargebacks and returns exceed the regular invoices for a given vendor. Many systems fail to recognize this situation and print negative checks, which is very poor form!

Check printing should be followed by a check register. Each check is listed on its own line, showing totals for invoices, discounts, and check amount. This listing takes the place of manual check registers or stubs. At the end of the listing, general ledger postings should be summarized, either to be posted automatically, if the system has a general ledger application implemented, or manually.

The payables system should also utilize an aged trial balance, which prints monthly and shows resolved items before they are purged from the system.

A cash requirements report is a very useful tool in a mechanized payables system. It augments the cash planning process by providing a list that totals all of the cash payments that would be required as of a certain date, entered by the person instigating the procedure. Such a report is of great assistance in forecasting the needs for cash and cash flow at certain dates in the future.

Vendor open items also need to be resolved with general ledger postings, in addition to the normal method of resolution by payment. Invoices will need to be written off and otherwise adjusted for various reasons.

General Ledger File Design

If transactions are to be posted automatically, the transactions should include a source code indicating that the transaction came from invoicing, cash receipts, accounts payable, or general journal sources. The source code and the date will provide a sufficient trail to lead back to the appropriate register.

A general journal facility must exist whereby postings may be made to various accounts directly, without going through any subsidiary acounts. The accounts themselves must exist and be appropriate for the posting being performed, and the debits must exactly equal the credits for every completed set of transactions. The operator ought to be informed of the cumulative balance of the transactions entered in each set and be able to review the entries made up to that point should the entries accidentally not balance to zero in order to identify the offending entry.

A trial balance should print at month-end. For each account, the opening balance should print; then the transactions for the month should print, usually sorted by date by source or by source by date for convenience. The monthly transactions should be totaled and the closing balance given for the account. The closing balance for a given month should agree with the opening balance for the coming month. Intermediate (perhaps departmental) totals should be given as required, and final totals should be printed at the end of the trial balance.

CHAPTER ELEVEN

Using a Computer Consultant

By now, you may be getting the idea that obtaining and implementing a successful computer system is a lot of work. And you are right. You may also be wondering whether it might not make sense to look for some help with the process.

Many businesspeople call upon computer consultants to help them in acquiring and implementing a computer system. There are ample reasons for this course of action. First, you simply may not have enough time. People who run a small business rarely find themselves with extra time on their hands. Second, you may feel (and rightly so) that you lack the expertise to accomplish all of the tasks that need doing. Third, you may wish to insure yourself against the problems that you know will occur if your own implementation efforts fall short of the mark.

Where Help Might Be Needed

The assistance of a consultant might be desired during the period of investigation and intensive fact-finding that takes place in the preparation of the RFP. Here an outsider may bring a fresh perspective and viewpoint to the effort to streamline manual systems and procedures.

Assistance may also be highly welcome in preparing long-range plans and objectives. Many entrepreneurial businesspeople, although highly effective, lack experience in this area.

Consultants with system design expertise can provide invaluable help in writing the RFP. They will be able to convert the lists of client problems and desired improvements into effective system solutions. As a result the client's position will be stronger and the client will be able to demand implementation of these solutions rather than seek solutions.

Consultants can be helpful in the selection of vendors once responses to the RFP have been received. Experienced consultants will be at home with the task of comparing and analyzing vendors' proposals and can identify additional information that has to be obtained from each.

Once the vendor choice has been made, the consultants may add expertise to the process of contract preparation and negotiation, an important and delicate area.

The one-time task of converting existing data to the new system can be handled by a consultant, who may have participated in many such conversions. Staff training also can be managed by the consultant. Testing programs is another area in which the consultant is likely to be of considerable assistance.

Finally, the consultant may be hired as an insurance policy of sorts to guarantee that none of these efforts bogs down. It is generally more expensive and difficult to find help when you're in the middle of a big mess.

Reasons Not to Use a Consultant

Certain motivations for using a consultant are self-defeating. Test your own motives against this list. Don't hire a consultant:

- to do all of the work himself
- to take the blame if things go wrong
- to agree with everything you say
- to wave a wand
- who has no experience with similar problems
- without checking his references very carefully
- who can't listen well
- who talks about other clients' confidential matters
- who has no references because they're "confidential"

Are Consultants Expensive?

Consultants generally quote "per diems," or daily rates. The work day is usually seven, seven and one-half, or eight hours. Per diems sound expensive. Bear in mind, however, when using consultants that the company does not have to pay for the consultant's social security, life and hospital insurance, profit-sharing, or pension benefits. Most consultants are not paid for nonwork time, such as sick or personal days, vacation, or holidays. Consultants run the risk that they may not be paid if their work is considered grossly unsatisfactory. Employees, on the other hand, usually receive compensation for time absent and termination pay if fired for unsatisfactory work. Finally, consultants often provide their own secretarial and support staff, services that are typically provided to in-house employees.

All this is not to argue that every consultant at every rate is a bargain but just to point out that quoted rates may not actually be as expensive as they sound. Indeed, in the case of functions that are performed only once, it is often far cheaper to hire a consultant than to hire in-house staff to do the same task.

Locating Good Computer Consultants

The search for the right consultant can take you to a number of places.

The major management consulting firms handle various types of computer consulting assignments. Their clients usually come from *Fortune*'s 500. Depending upon the size of your problem and your pocketbook, such firms may be considered a resource. Be sure the personnel have hands-on experience.

Public accounting firms have become increasingly interested in the business computer marketplace and have established computer consulting departments. They serve a wider range of clients than do management consulting firms and may be more interested in servicing a modest business.

Be sure with both management consulting and accounting firms to establish who actually will be performing the consulting services for you. In large, structured organizations such as these there is a tendency for the more seasoned people to write the proposals that land the clients and for the actual consulting to be done by relatively inexperienced staff members.

Self-employed consultants are frequently found in the computer field. These individuals have usually been employed previously by consulting or accounting firms, software houses, or manufacturers and have gone out on their own. They are somewhat more difficult to locate than are large firms providing computer consulting services.

Prospective users of consultants may obtain recommendations from equipment manufacturers. This may be a very effective way to locate the right consultant, especially if it is important to have expertise with a particular piece of equipment. On the other hand, the client who has not yet made an equipment decision may find that the manufacturer's referral leads to a conflict of interest on the part of the consultant. The consultant, whose livelihood may depend in large part upon referrals, may be reluctant to choose a different brand of hardware from that manufactured by his benefactor. Some manufacturers make conflicts of interest even stronger by offering finders' fees to parties such as consultants who make customer introductions that culminate in an equipment sale. An ethical consultant will accept no remuneration except from his client.

Computer trade associations keep lists of consultants and specialists. These lists are often maintained by geographical location and by specialty. Rarely does a formal accreditation process occur in preparing these lists, so that a consultant's being mentioned on one means little more than activity in the field for a fairly long time.

The best way to locate a consultant is through references from other companies in a similar business. If your industry has a trade association or other channel in which you have the opportunity to meet businesspeople with similar problems, make extensive inquiries about the use of computer consultants there. Ask neighbors and community contacts, too, as personal references are usually the most reliable.

Choosing the Right Consultant

After you have obtained the names of several potential consultants, a final choice has to be made. There a number of elements to consider in making the final choice. First, identify those whose experience matches your problem most closely. If your system will be oriented heavily toward inventory component control, a consultant who has never implemented an inventory system is not likely to be very useful. While the match does not have to be a complete one, the closer the consultant's expertise to your needs, the more useful the relationship.

Look for the best possible working relationship. Implementing computer systems can be tense and difficult. A fair amount of money, time, and effort are involved, as well as peoples' careers and reputations. You want a consultant with whom you can work well. This means different things to different people but must include open communications between you. Does each of you hear what the other is trying to say? There must also be the willingness of each to accept constructive criticism. Look for the same personal relationship that you would like to have with a trusted staff assistant.

The consultant you choose must have integrity and trustworthiness. He will eventually have access to every area of your business. If your industry is one in which competitors are highly interested in each other's dealings, this point becomes critical. If the consultant happens to have obtained the expertise you need while working for your competitor, address the issue with him. You should be able to come to some sort of arrangement in which your confidential information is protected, his expertise is used to advantage, and the previous client's dealings are treated with respect as well.

Check consultants' references carefully: call each and every one. Remember that the individual you contact may be reluctant to volunteer information that makes him appear to have made a selection error! Ask specific questions—"Should I continue to consider other consultants?" and "Would you use this consultant again?" Listen carefully for signs of lukewarm praise. It helps to put yourself in the other user's place.

How to Work with a Consultant

The consultant will be able to do his best if he has complete sponsorship from you. You yourself should give him a personal introduction to every staff member with whom he will be working, including outside accountants and legal counsel if necessary. He should also be given as much information about the company as you can gather before he starts work so that he will be informed and asking good questions when he begins.

Be specific about your objectives for the consultant. If possible, prepare a written agreement so that there is no doubt in anyone's mind about the tasks he is to perform.

Assign a liaison person within your company to work with the consultant. This will help preserve the results of his efforts after he is gone.

Finally, have frequent meetings and review sessions and go over the status of unfinished tasks often. Set deadlines by which objectives will be met. The more specific you can be about what needs to be done, the more likely it is that the consultant will prove beneficial.

CHAPTER TWELVE

Different Kinds of Vendors

In the heyday of large batch and mainframe computers, manufacturers could throw in software and custom programming as the prices of the systems themselves were very large, often in the millions of dollars. Things are very different in today's minicomputer market. System prices are well under $100,000 for very large minicomputers and substantially less for smaller ones, as prices drop steadily. No manufacturer finds it economically feasible to include custom programing.

Some manufacturers have created packages for applications common to numerous buyers, such as accounts payable and general ledger. Others have attempted to boost their marketing and sales appeal by providing sophisticated data base management systems, report generators, query languages, word processing packages, and enhanced languages. All of these features attempt to address the question of providing custom software by making the process of preparing it more productive.

But the fact remains that the business of preparing custom software for minicomputers has been left to small, local vendors by the economics of the minicomputer business. Companies that do not want to deal with small vendors in acquiring software have the choice of developing their own software or facing some very limited alternatives.

There are several species of this genus of vendor.

The "software (only) house" is just that. It provides analysis, consulting, and programming services. It does not sell hardware. It may or may not receive financial encouragement from hardware salespeople, depending upon the supply and demand of software houses and/or customers in a particular geographic area. Normally such a business will have targeted a small group of manufacturers for whose equipment they will write software, as it is extremely expensive to be up-to-date on a number of different manufacturers' hardware. These software companies generally are located through manufacturer recommendations, through word of mouth, through local direct mail campaigns, and occasionally through marketing efforts at computer or industry conferences. Companies utilizing such vendors will find themselves in a three-party arrangement of hardware vendor, software vendor, and themselves.

The "distributor" represents a particular manufacturer in a geographic territory. He arranges a hardware discount with the manufacturer that depends upon the volume of systems he can move. He generally undertakes to do a customer's custom software and also provides packages for less customized applications. He frequently offers a "turnkey" or all-in-one price to the customer. His profit margins then are made up partially from the difference between the hardware list price and the discounted price he pays for the equipment and partially from any profits that result directly from the software process. With such a vendor and the typical turnkey arrangement, the company may nevertheless have legal recourse to the manufacturer as well as the distributor in case of dissatisfaction.

The term OEM stands for "original equipment manufacturer" and is a misnomer. In the minicomputer marketplace, OEM means a company that has assembled a computer system using the peripherals and processors of different manufacturers. The OEM vendor generally contributes the operating system and sometimes a maintenance capability as his value added to the equipment. The customer deals only with the OEM and has no recourse to the manufacturers of the equipment. Turnkey arrangements are common. The vendor makes his profit on the spread between the bulk prices he pays for components and the prices he charges for systems. Unlike the distributor, he is able to set his own list price. These arrangements are almost always localized in particular geographic areas.

There are several variations on these themes, but certain generalizations can be made. First, the equipment manufacturer will seldom if ever get involved in preparing custom programming. If done, it is usually at a price additional to the equipment price;

moreover, such a service is provided by a local or a branch office, not nationally. Even package programs are difficult to obtain from manufacturers. Minicomputer manufacturers do not want to be in the software business. Second, the sources for software generally will be small companies. The larger accounting firms seem to be entering the field recently, providing packages for the simpler applications and offering to customize them at a price (perhaps not a fixed price). To some extent, this trend will depend upon the progress that manufacturers are able to make in rendering the programming process more productive. It will depend also upon the supply of qualified programming personnel. The present supply is short, and the larger firms, with their smaller salaries, may not be able to attract the people necessary to continue this kind of effort.

No matter which type of vendor is being investigated, it is important to take a "show me" attitude in dealing with them.

First, a vendor should be specifically asked to include information about your system in his proposal so that you can judge his understanding of your RFP. Often vendors will totally misunderstand a major facet of your system, and there is no way of knowing that this has happened unless you demand feedback from them.

Second, there is every reason to ask to be shown some evidence of a vendor's capabilities and experience in what you need done. Say, "Take me to one of your happy customers for whom you did something like what I want." Go to that customer's business, stay quite a while, and ask lots of questions. Interview the operators and management of that system; buy them lunch and ask probing questions in such a way that they can admit they made a mistake.

Third, ask the vendor to perform on the spot. Have the programmers brought out to take the programming test and discuss their capabilities with you. If some aspect of your proposed system especially worries you, ask them to work up a demonstration that will put your mind at ease. The worst they can say is no, and most won't do that.

In general, don't be too shy, gracious, or polite (not that outright rudeness is being recommended here) in asking to see real evidence from a vendor that his system is the right one for you. The vendor decision is an important one. You will have to live with the results for a long time. Be definite and forceful in expressing your desire to make as good a decision as possible and to have as much information as you need.

CHAPTER THIRTEEN

Evaluating Vendors' Proposals

At long last, the RFP is finished and mailed out to prospective vendors. And finally, the vendor proposals begin to be received. Some are really quite impressive to look at, in fancy binders with four-color brochures showing lovely young women operating fancy equipment.

As you view the stack of proposals, the enormity of the task about to be performed may overwhelm you. Which proposal is the right one for you? Which one would be seriously wrong? How can you tell the difference?

It would be nice to have a black box into which you could feed each proposal in turn. When they had all gone in, a hand would emerge from the box, bearing a card identifying the right choice. Until the black box is invented, we need a disciplined approach to detailed analysis of the various alternatives.

Making a Grid

There is nothing sophisticated or magic about using a grid to compare a number of alternatives. The alternatives are placed along the tops of the pages of the grid. The factors being compared are listed down the left edges of the pages. Thus, for each alternative, the appropriate facts are laid out vertically, making them easy to compare.

Identifying the factors that need to be compared is the hardest thing about constructing a grid. This chapter describes a number of the factors that should be included in a grid that will be useful in evaluating vendor proposals.

The Grid Process May Surprise You

The idea that answering a group of questions about each alternative might be illuminating may seem farfetched. And yet, the process never fails to surprise those who go through it. The first surprise is the number of questions that go virtually unaddressed in almost all proposals, despite the elegant appearance of some of them. It is the unusual proposal, indeed, that answers all of the questions on the grid. The second surprise is that your initial impressions of the vendors and their proposals will be permanently altered once the grid has been completed. The proposal that originally seemed best will rarely occupy that position ultimately. Another proposal, which did not make an excellent first impression, will look more attractive after the grid is finished. This has been the experience of most grid users.

In many instances, the grid process will immediately pick out one alternative as best. But even when the choice is not entirely clear-cut, several of the vendors will have been eliminated definitively in the process. The issues that differentiate the remaining vendors will be well defined, and the elements of the decision to be made will be clear to all participants.

Decisionmaking is considerably improved and simplified as a result of the grid process.

The Contents of the Grid

You may want to construct your own grid, emphasizing the elements that are important to the success of your computer system. What is central to the grid process is that a disciplined checklist of factors to be considered be developed and completed for each vendor.

The grid given here includes factors that you should consider for your grid. The factors are presented first in outline form and then described individually for further clarification.

The Structure of the Grid

Factors	Alternative A	Alternative B . . . Alternative Z
I. General Background		
A. In-house operator expertise		
B. In-house programming expertise		
C. Demonstrations and visits		
D. Local backup		
II. Hardware Factors		
A. Name of system		
B. Manufacturer(s) of system		
C. Delivery date of first system		
D. Number delivered to date		
E. Operating temperature range		
F. Operating humidity range		
G. Configuration as proposed		
1. Central processing unit (in characters)		
2. Disk storage (in million characters)		
a. Fixed		
b. Removable		
3. Magnetic tape drives (in inches per second and bits per inch)		
4. Number of terminals		

(cont.)

The Structure of the Grid *(cont.)*

	Alternative A	Alternative B . . .	Alternative Z
5. Communications devices			
6. Printer(s)			
7. Other entry devices			
8. Other output devices			
H. Expansion potential of proposed hardware			
1. Central processing unit			
2. Disk storage			
a. Fixed			
b. Removable			
3. Magnetic tape drives			
4. Number of terminals			
5. Communications devices			
6. Printer(s)			
7. Other entry devices			
8. Other output devices			
9. Additional memory required per new terminal			
I. Upgradable to bigger system (model)			
J. Ease of upgrading			
K. Purchase price			
1. As proposed			
2. As adjusted for common configuration			

L. Maintenance
   1. Provided by
   2. Cost per month
   3. Terms of service
   4. Duration of contract

III. Hardware Vendor Factors
   A. Date established
   B. Number of employees
   C. Gross sales
   D. Net earnings
   E. Ownership
   F. Percentage of gross sales derived from data processing sales and services.
   G. Number of U.S. sales/service offices
   H. Strength of nearest sales/service office
   I. User references
   J. Indications of commitment to success of end user systems
   K. Support given to maintenance vendor

IV. Systems Software
   A. Operating system
   B. Mode of operation
   C. Responsibility for operating system maintenance
   D. Efficiency of file structures
   E. Flexibility of file manipulations
   F. Languages(s) available

(cont.)

The Structure of the Grid *(cont.)*

	Alternative A	Alternative B . . .	Alternative Z
G. Ease of expansion			
H. Software features			
1. Report generator			
2. Text editor			
3. Word processing			
4. Other features			
I. Communications facilities			
V. Software Vendor Factors			
A. Date established			
B. Number of employees			
C. Gross sales			
D. Net earnings			
E. Ownership			
F. Percentage of gross sales derived from data processing sales and services			
G. Number of U.S. sales/service offices			
H. Strength of nearest sales/service office			
I. Total number of systems installed			
J. Number of similar systems installed			
K. User references			

L. Applications
   1. Areas included in proposal; price for each if available
   2. Understanding shown in proposal and other encounters
   3. Training included
   4. Conversion assistance included
   5. Documentation included

M. Software price

N. Software warranty period

O. Provisions for postwarranty maintenance of software

P. Second source assistance possibilities

VI. Financial Considerations

A. Financial stability of hardware vendor

B. Financial stability of software vendor

C. Financial stability of maintenance vendor

D. Contract terms
   1. Deposit required on signing contract
   2. Payment required on approval of programming specifications
   3. Payment required after satisfactory demonstration of software
   4. Payment required upon delivery of hardware
   5. Payment required after installation of application(s) module(s)

E. Total purchase price

F. Terms of refund of deposit

(cont.)

The Structure of the Grid *(cont.)*

	Alternative A	Alternative B . . . Alternative Z
G. Rental arrangements		
H. Available lease arrangements		
1. Term of lease		
2. Monthly payments		
3. Identity of lessor		
4. Buyout provisions at expiration of lease		

I. General Background

A. Is in-house operator expertise required to operate the system? The best systems are designed for foolproof operation by relatively untrained staff members. On a visit to the site of another customer of the prospective vendor, observe the operators of the keyboard entry devices. Frequently it will also be easy to inquire about their level of previous experience. Ideally, they will be the same personnel who previously performed the same functions (such as order taking) manually and will not have had prior keyboard data entry experience or even strong typing skills.

B. Is programming or other data processing experience required on the part of the system supervisor? This, too, can be gleaned from visiting a customer's site. If documentation and run-time instructions have been well prepared, and good training has taken place, it should not have been necessary to hire a trained data processor to supervise the system. The individual placed in charge of the system may have become much more knowledgeable about data processing as a result of his new supervisory responsibilities, however, so that a direct question may be necessary.

C. Summarize the findings of visits to customer sites and demonstrations of system capabilities. Was the demonstration sufficient to provide a clear visualization of the possibilities for your future system, or was it impossible to imagine how the system might work? Did the systems appear to be performing the objectives for which they were designed? Were the customers satisfied or enthusiastic?

D. Is local backup available in the event of protracted down time? Many users enjoy the security of knowing that there is another system they could use in the event of a serious malfunction of their own system. Frequently manufacturers will offer this kind of accommodation at their sales office or demonstration site. Occasionally two customers with similar configurations will have reciprocal arrangements, with each agreeing to make their system available to the other on an off-hours basis should the need arise. While the actual use of such privileges is rare, knowing that they exist is reassuring.

II. Hardware Factors

A. The manufacturer's name or model number of the system should be given.
B. The name of the manufacturer is given. If the system is a combination of components from different manufacturers, mention the names of the manufacturers of the major components, such as the CPU, disk drives, printer, and CRTs.
C. Obtain the delivery date for the first such system.
D. Obtain the number of such systems delivered to date.
E. Determine the temperature range in which the most demanding component will operate successfully. This information is usually contained in the manufacturer's physical installation manual.
F. Determine the humidity range in which the most demanding component will operate successfully. This question and the previous one should remind you to review your plans for the equipment site and analyze the environmental requirements (see Chapter 6 for a discussion of this subject).
G. Enter the amounts and sizes of the various components being proposed (see Chapter 3 for a review of components).

1. Central processing unit. This is usually expressed as some number of K.
2. Disk storage. This is usually expressed as some number of million characters and is broken down by storage that is:
   a. Fixed
   b. Removable
3. Magnetic tape drives. Mention the number of drives being proposed and their speed (in terms of inches per second) and density (in terms of bits per inch).
4. Number of terminals. Mention here the number of cathode ray tube (CRT) terminals being proposed.
5. Communications devices. Mention here any remote devices being proposed.
6. Printer(s). Mention here each printer being proposed and its rated speed in terms of characters per second or lines per minute. Mention also any special printing features such as uppercase-lowercase or special type fonts.

7. Other entry devices. Mention here any other devices being proposed to enter data into the system; for example, optical or mark-sense readers, cassettes, or diskettes.
8. Other output devices. Mention here any other devices being proposed for output purposes; for example, plotters, cassettes, or diskettes.

H. Determine the maximum expansion potential for each category of component. This information can usually be provided by the hardware salesperson, if not supplied in the proposal. Use the same terms of reference given above.

   1. Central processing unit.
   2. Disk storage
      a. Fixed
      b. Removable
   3. Magnetic tape drives
   4. Number of terminals
   5. Communications devices
   6. Printer(s)
   7. Other entry devices
   8. Other output devices
   9. Is additional memory required when adding terminals (see Chapter 3)? If so, at what cost?

I. Some manufacturers limit the expansion potential of particular models but offer the option to upgrade to the next higher model in their product line. If this is the case, obtain the name of the upgrade model.

J. Determine at the same time the effort and expense required to accomplish such an upgrade. Ask specifically whether reprogramming is required and whether some proposed hardware components might become obsolete in the process of upgrading.

K. The purchase price of the hardware is invariably included in each vendor's proposal. Vendors will propose varying configurations of hardware, however, which makes a direct comparison of purchase prices misleading.

   1. Enter the purchase price for the proposed configuration.

2. Determine the purchase price for a "common" configuration, as follows: Construct a configuration that is not substantially different from each of the proposed configurations. For example, if vendors proposed two, three, and four terminals, define the common configuration to be three terminals. If vendors proposed 30, 40, and 50 million characters of disk storage, include 40 million in the common configuration. Once the common configuration has been developed, contact each hardware vendor and ask for list prices for the common configuration. (The vendor's proposal stays unchanged.) By obtaining prices from each vendor for a common configuration, actual price differences may be identified more easily. You may be surprised at the similarity in prices, as marketing strategies among the major minicomputer manufacturers are fiercely competitive. The existing differences will probably be the result of varying required amounts of memory to support a given number of peripheral devices on each system.

L. Maintenance arrangements should have been included in the proposal. Repairs and preventive maintenance are commonly contracted for at a fixed monthly fee, usually somewhat less than one percent of the purchase price. The following facts should be included.

1. Name of provider or maintenance services
2. Cost per month
3. Terms of service, including time promised to respond to service calls and number of hours and days of the week covered.
4. Length of contract term. In inflationary times, the longer the term of a fixed fee contract, the better.

III. Hardware Vendor Factors

Some basic information about each hardware vendor should be assembled. This information is commonly available in the vendor's annual report and in standard industry references. While assembling this material for the very large manufacturers may seem foolish, bear in mind that several major computer manufacturers (RCA, XDS, GE) have left the computer field since the mid-sixties!

A. Obtain the date when the vendor firm was established.
B. Obtain the current number of employees.
C. Obtain the current level of gross sales.
D. Obtain the current level of net earnings.
E. Specify the ownership of the company. If public, specify the exchange on which the security is traded.
F. Determine the percentage of gross sales derived from data processing sales and services.
G. Obtain the number of U.S. sales/service offices.
H. Determine the strength of the nearest sales/service office.
I. Contact all possible current users of the equipment. Concentrate particularly on system reliability, maintenance response time, and cooperation from the branch office.
J. If possible, determine the hardware vendor's level of commitment to the success of the end final users' systems. Try to assess the relationship and level of cooperation between the hardware and software vendors. Neither one can create a successful system without the assistance of the other.
K. Determine the hardware vendor's level of cooperation with the maintenance vendor (if a different party). Try to assess the maintenance vendor's (or local service office's) reputation for carrying adequate stock levels of common replacement parts.

IV. Systems Software

A. Obtain the exact name of the operating system (see Chapter 4 for a review of operating system concepts) being proposed for the hardware.
B. Determine its intended mode of operation. In other words, is the system set up to process interactively or in batch mode?
C. Determine which party is responsible for maintenance of the operating system. Most operating systems have periodic problems. The manufacturers issue "patches" (bug fixes), improvements, and occasionally entirely new versions of the operating system. In some situations, the hardware vendor will handle these matters; in other cases they will be the responsibility of the software vendor.

D. If possible, determine whether the operating system incorporates an efficient file structure. This may not be easy for a person without data processing background to do. If the term "variable length records" has been used in describing the way in which data is stored in the system, you could judge it to be relatively efficient. This means that data that varies in length takes up only the space that each individual element requires, rather than a fixed block of space sufficient to hold all possible lengths of data. In the average name and address file a savings of 30 percent of disk space is possible if variable length records are used to advantage. In the absence of variable length records, other techniques may be used to store data efficiently.

E. The relative flexibility of file manipulations may also be a difficult factor for the non–data processing oriented person to evaluate. Operating systems generally provide "utility" programs that are used to manipulate and transfer information within the system. Some utility functions are more versatile than others. Consultants and systems analysts who work with different file structures and utility programs will be useful in answering this and the previous question.

F. Determine which languages are available for use on the system (see Chapter 4 for an overview of programming languages). If the use of one language or another requires an extra payment, indicate that as well.

G. The ease with which software permits hardware expansion must be determined. This information is unlikely to be in the proposals and may require specific questioning. Be aware in forming your questions that some operating systems software limits hardware expansion though the hardware per se might not have such limitations.

H. The presence (or absence) of special features in the systems software may be a very important aspect of vendor selection. Manufacturers are becoming aware of the demand for these special features and are increasingly including them. The three special features mentioned here will definitely become standard offerings from all manufacturers in the 1980s so attractive is their potential to almost all computer system users. The informed user would be wise to try to obtain a system with these features.

1. Report generator. This feature was described in

Chapter 4. In simple terms, it enables the non–data processing oriented user to draw additional reports from his own data without the help of a programmer. Its presence, while making all of the data in the system available and of direct use to its user, also considerably improves programmer productivity during the system development stages. The benefits that a facile report generator can provide to its user are enormous!

2. Text editor. This feature allows the users of the system to prepare textual materials at the terminal. It generally allows the user to key in new text, make corrections easily with minimal keying, search for and change specific text to other text, and rearrange sentences, paragraphs, and entire sections easily. In an environment where text is prepared, printed, edited, reprinted, re-edited, reprinted again, and so on, the convenience afforded by a text editor is enormous. Text editors are also frequently used to enter and modify programming code on the system.
3. Word processing. This feature extends the abilities of text editing and facilitates letter writing, document preparation, and correspondence. Some word processing applications have the ability to utilize names and addresses from master files and to vary the format of a document based upon logical conditions. For example, a letter writing system might send an aggressive letter to a customer with a large very overdue balance and a milder letter to a customer whose account was less delinquent. Sophisticated applications utilize quality uppercase-lowercase printers.
4. Other special features exist and are usually developed for the unique needs of a particular industry.

I. Communications facilities are frequently offered as a part of systems software. Many software vendors, taking advantage of this trend, now are offering remote diagnostic and debugging services to their customers on a regular basis. This means that your software vendor has access to your system through telephone communications lines and can inspect and correct problems from his location. Ask if this capability is present. If so, it will prove extremely convenient and useful. Once the system is completed, the same facility can be used to allow executives to communicate with the system through terminals in their homes or from remote offices.

V. Software Vendor Factors

This section may not apply if the hardware and software vendors are the same party or if your company is planning to create its own software. If there is a software vendor, corporate information should be assembled as it was for the hardware vendor and should include:

A. Date established
B. Number of employees
C. Gross sales
D. Net earnings
E. Ownership
F. Percentage of gross sales derived from data processing sales and services
G. Number of U.S. sales/service offices
H. Strength of nearest sales/service office

As a rule, software firms are smaller and financially weaker than hardware vendors. This would follow since establishing a software firm takes a great deal less capital than starting a hardware manufacturing company! Some of the above information may be difficult to obtain for software firms. However, they should be willing to provide evidence of financial stability if requested directly.

I. Find out the total number of systems installed by the firm.
J. Determine how many of these systems are similar in some degree to the system you would like installed. While these systems may not be in your industry, they may involve similar elements of design, such as being heavily oriented toward job costing, back order control, or direct mail marketing.
K. Check out user references extensively and indicate a summary

of the results. Visit as many of the sites of the significant vendors as possible.

L. The applications that the software vendor is proposing to computerize should be reviewed, with respect to the following considerations:

1. List each application the vendor has proposed to include. Indicate the price for the application, if priced separately. Indicate also applications that will not be included by the vendor.
2. Judge how much understanding the vendor has shown of the objectives to be met in each application. Judge both material presented in the proposal and any demonstrations or discussions that may have occurred. Evaluating the vendor's level of understanding of the problems at hand is critical for it indicates how well the communications process may (or may not) be working between you and the vendor. Most of the difficulties users encounter with their computer systems generally are the result of the vendor's failure to understand what needs to be done rather than his inability to do it.
3. Evaluate the quality and quantity of the training the vendor proposes to provide. Inquire of previous customers as to whether the training they received was timely and adequate.
4. Evaluate the level of conversion assistance that the vendor proposes to provide. Determine the cost of such assistance if it has not been included in the overall price or specifically spelled out in the proposal.
5. Evaluate the quality of the documentation that is to be provided. Ask to see the documentation at an existing customer's site; evaluate it for clarity and completeness; ask the customer whether it is accurate and up-to-date!

M. List the total software price. Remember in comparing vendors' prices that different vendors may include varying applications, as mentioned above.

N. Determine how long the vendor is willing to warrant his work to be free from defects (i.e., he will fix problems free during that period). To give no warranty is unreasonable. Three to six months is common, and a year is excellent. Beyond that point, a long warranty begins to seem less than credible. One vendor promised his customers a lifetime warranty; few asked whose lifetime that meant. The lifetime in question turned out to be the vendor's, which ended within three years!

O. Once the warranty has expired, is there provision for follow-on software maintenance? Indicate here the charges and conditions for postwarranty efforts. Asking other customers what their experience has been can be extremely helpful. They may tell you that the vendor is gracious about repairing program defects long after the official warranty period has expired, as he values a good working relationship and has sincere concern that the system be free from bugs! Their experience may also indicate a nickel and diming relationship, wherein every issue is hotly contested and bugs are fixed reluctantly or at great expense.

P. Determine whether software extensions and modifications after the warranty has expired can be performed by another vendor. In some situations, the customer has no choice but to continue with the original vendor either because the programming languages or procedures used were so esoteric that he cannot locate a capable second source vendor or (more commonly) because the documentation and instructions for the system are inadequate and no one else knows how the system works! This can be a most unfortunate situation indeed, especially when the relationship between the customer and the vendor has deteriorated. Just as you might not want to buy a car that only one mechanic can fix, you should also avoid a computer system that only a single vendor can repair, maintain, and enhance.

VI. Financial Considerations

A. The stability of the hardware vendor is a factor to be considered if the vendor is not one of the major vendors or has a shaky financial history. Yes, there is always the risk that another major vendor will leave the marketplace, and that development probably would not be easy to predict with even the most sophisticated analysis. But bear in mind what happened to the customers of the large vendors who did discontinue their computer businesses. These customers were not alone; the manufacturers had virtually thousands of systems in their installed customer bases. A customer base of such magnitude has real economic value and in each case was sold to or absorbed by another company. So while the customers involved certainly were inconvenienced and unhappy about the turn of events, they had time to regroup and convert to other hardware and were neither immediately nor disastrously denied the ability to process on their equipment. As with any capital expenditure such as a computer system, it is important to deal with stable, solid, reputable vendors.

B. The stability of the software vendor is a much more critical factor. As the majority of software firms are much smaller and less well capitalized than the major hardware vendors, there is a real risk that the vendor may find himself unable to complete your system or expend the kind of effort on it that you would like. Being left with an unfinished system is like having a car without gas. Smallness in a software firm is to some a desirable feature, as software is still considered to be an art rather than a science. They feel that as a software firm grows larger, its quality and performance are likely to decline. Software is difficult to produce in an assembly line fashion. Management problems and demands in a software firm tend to grow geometrically as size grows arithmetically! Quality and size may be mutually exclusive here. There is a period of maximum vulnerability in your dealings with a software vendor that occurs when most of the planning and design of the future system have been completed but not adequately documented and programming is incomplete. During that vulnerable period, much effort and time will have been lost if the vendor is unable to continue, as the work is left unfinished with incomplete indications as to how it should be finished. You can lessen your financial exposure should this happen by tying your payments to "deliverables," or finished, documented modules of work. It is more difficult to protect yourself against delays and loss of momentum, which also have an eventual cost to you. Having a consultant assist the vendor during the planning and design stages will lessen your vulnerability, as some of the knowledge will then be retained by your representative. Insisting upon written minutes of meetings, preliminary specifications, and documentation that stays as current as possible will also lessen such difficulties. You should satisfy yourself that the software vendor has sufficient resources to carry you well past the period of vulnerability. Once the programs are complete, bug-free, and documented, and you have the freedom to utilize a second source, you will be much less at his mercy.

C. The financial stability of the maintenance vendor also has to be considered. Should the vendor have less than ideal financial stability, the safest course is to locate alternative sources of maintenance (they usually exist) before committing to that alternative vendor.

D. Review and list the contract terms that each vendor proposes. One way to minimize financial risk is to link payment to performance. Break up the total payment into stages such as listed below.

   1. Deposit required on signing contract. This is common.
   2. Payment required upon specification approval. An acceptable specification can be considered a deliverable as it constitutes good documentation and would be useful in the event of the vendor's demise.
   3. Payment required after satisfactory demonstration of software.
   4. Payment required upon delivery of hardware.
   5. Payment required after installation of application module(s).

   Payments may be arranged in other fashions but should be consistent with the goals and objectives of the company.

E. List the total purchase price, combining hardware and software prices.

F. List the conditions and terms under which any deposits or payments would be refundable.

G. List any provisions that exist for system rental, giving monthly amounts and any conditions that apply.

H. List any lease provisions that may be proposed, including the following.

   1. Term of lease
   2. Monthly payment amount. Does it include maintenance?

3. Identity and description of the lessor.
4. Buyout provisions at expiration of lease.

CHAPTER FOURTEEN

The Computer Contract

When the time comes for your company to negotiate and draft a contract with the computer vendor of your choice, you are well advised to make generous use of the most competent legal counsel you can find! This chapter is in no way meant to substitute for such assistance. It is meant, however, to provide you and your attorney with some help in contract preparation by reviewing a number of subjects and areas of negotiation that may be germane.

It has been said that the test of a successful contract is that no one ever looks at it afterward. In other words, the parties find themselves in basic agreement and do not feel the need to refer to the contract's provisions in seeking redress. The converse of this claim would be that a contract is unsuccesful if it is reviewed frequently and its provisions are quoted as threats by one party to the other. While there is obviously no way to prove or disprove these contentions here, it stands to reason that a contract drawn up in an atomsphere of careful forethought and that anticipates and resolves most logical conflicts in advance should lessen the chance of legal problems later. Here, then, I attempt to identify the major areas of discussion and negotiation that should be pursued by the company and the vendor during the period of contract preparation. Once the parties have agreed in principle to the major concepts involved, the precise wording of the agreement should be left to the lawyers!

The Computer System

All computer contracts, in their introductory section, will identify and describe the nature and scope of the transaction as well as the general nature of the computer system. The parties involved will be specified and the major elements of hardware and software will be identified either directly or through reference to various attachments and schedules. Finally, the purchase, lease, or rental price is quoted, as are the major terms of the transaction.

It is important that the contract clearly describe the computer system the company expects to obtain. For this reason, the RFP is frequently included in its entirety as an attachment to the contract. This is an excellent idea, as it commits both parties to agreeing that the contract contains a valid description of the goals and objectives that the desired system should meet. Attaching the RFP also saves substantial time and expense in the preparation of the contract, which otherwise would have to discuss the particular applications, goals, and objectives that the RFP normally contains. (This use of the RFP is another good reason for writing one!)

The "implementation schedule" is another logical attachment to the contract. This document, normally prepared with the assistance of both parties, spells out a specific schedule for the implementation of all aspects and applications of the system. The planning process that goes into preparing the implementation schedule is a significant one, requiring a great deal of cooperation and effort from the parties. Many subjects must be covered and numerous points negotiated. During this stage some vendor-company relationships may run into difficulty, as there is an inherent conflict of interest between the two parties with respect to the implementation schedule. The company wants its system developed and delivered in as little time as is consistent with a high quality result—and perhaps at the expense of the vendor's commitment to other projects. The vendor, on the other hand, wants enough time so as not to risk failing to follow the schedule and so as to be able to honor his existing commitments as well. Accordingly, the give-and-take process that has to go on during the preparation of the implementation schedule may sound the death knell of the fledgling vendor-company relationship. The company should be especially attuned to the nature of the working relationship at this stage and should give serious consideration to terminating the relationship if the parties are having real difficulty agreeing to the schedule. Once the implementation schedule has been completed, it should be attached to the contract. Without this specific list of objectives to be accomplished within specific time frames, it would be very difficult indeed to establish the fact that a schedule had not been adhered to.

Further attachments to the contract may include sales materials, vendor proposal materials, and manufacturers' literature. These items should be appended to the contract as they provide information that indicates what the company's expectations and understandings were at the time of purchase. Some contracts have annexed the entire collection of vendor proposal and correspondence materials. This documentation may be very useful in the event of litigation and it certainly is not difficult to assemble.

The contract may also mention the "detailed system specifications," a document the company and the vendor expect to produce together in the future. The expectation that this document will be a joint effort should be made clear. To insure that the effort remains a joint one, the company could acknowledge its understanding of the natural conflicts among speed, accuracy, and cost in the design and operation of a system and could secure the vendor's commitment that judgments among these alternatives will be made jointly during the preparation of the detailed system specifications.

System Delivery Provisions

In some turnkey contracts, the vendor agrees to implement the entire system in accordance with the implementation schedule. If the schedule is not adhered to, the entire agreement is considered canceled; the vendor is to remove whatever hardware was delivered and refund all monies paid up to that point. This may sound like a very generous, almost foolhardy, offer by a vendor and yet the offer is not as generous as a first glance suggests. The vendor, in making the offer, has the benefit of experience with the realities of system implementation. The company, if convinced that quality work is being done in good faith, is very unlikely to bring a halt to the entire system development process if there are minor delays in implementation. After all, the company would have to renew its vendor search and start again with another vendor—which is not a pleasant alternative. Obviously this reasoning does not shift over into major delays of implementation and of course does not apply when poor work is being done. But in the case of a satisfactory company-vendor relationship, where good work is being performed and appreciated, it is in a company's best interests to forgive minor delays in the implementation schedule. At the same time, the company can retain its right to terminate the agreement if it wishes to do so.

Responsibility for developing the detailed system specifications should be discussed in detail in the contract. For example, the company and its consultants may have chosen to bear primary responsibility for the development of these specifications under the theory of asking for what you want instead of taking what you get. The vendor may then have been asked in the agreement to cooperate with the company in providing advice and assistance. This arrangement may not be possible and/or desirable in every situation but should be a function of a company's ability and desire to shoulder such responsibility itself.

The contract may state that the vendor is responsible for determining whether the specifications are technically workable and must notify the company if they are not. In one contract, the vendor was charged with implementing features that might be only implied by the specifications. This may be somewhat confusing and an example will help. Let's say that a sample report layout in the specifications included a fact such as the date of last invoice; the vendor would then be responsible for making sure that the date of last invoice was made available by the system for printing on that report.

Providing for a "monthly tasks memorandum" is an excellent idea, as well as good management practice. This kind of provision can require that company and vendor representatives meet at least monthly and prepare a memorandum, initialed by both parties, that outlines their upcoming responsibilities. Periods of major software development can be tense and difficult times for all concerned. Often worries over what remains to be done eclipse acknowledgment of what has been accomplished already. Frequently, the tasks being worked on are of such magnitude that long periods can go by without anything appearing to have been totally finished. Good communication between the parties may make the difference between the impression that nothing has been completed and the knowledge that meaningful, steady progress has been made. Regular meetings with coordinated records of priorities to be accomplished and documented results of accomplishments keep everyone abreast of the actual (rather than the perceived) status of each project. These meetings can also prevent the unfortunate situations that can occur when schedules begin to deteriorate.

Some attention should be given in the contract to the subject of program testing. Certainly, the site at which program testing will take place should be agreed upon. In one contract, it was established that program testing would take place initially at the vendor's location. In this way, machine delivery to the customer's location could be canceled or postponed until the results of the testing were satisfactory. It is important, particularly when *three* parties are involved (company, software vendor, and hardware vendor) to avoid a situation wherein the hardware is delivered before the software is usable. Even if only two parties are involved, the company might not want to waste its hardware warranty period by accepting hardware delivery before the software was usable. One solution is to specify in the contract that program testing will be performed on the vendor's system before authorization to ship the hardware to the company's premises can be given.

The contract can also specify that test transactions are to be provided by the company. This may seem unusual but it can be a very good idea. The subject of testing is discussed at greater length in Chapter 16. It is sufficient to say here that testing is generally more productive if done by people with a fresh perspective other than those who prepared the programs.

The vendor and the company should have agreed during the preparation of the implementation schedule on a time frame during which programming will be completed. The company can also agree in the contract that there is a minimum time period that the vendor will always be allowed for any programming task. This is a realistic concession on the part of the company: the vendor needs sufficient time to do a good job and giving this time is in the company's best interests. This fact is often overlooked in contract negotiations with vendors. Successful computer programming, as we have already discussed, takes time and effort. No one is well served if programming is done in a haphazard or slipshod manner.

The contract should set out the responsibilities for preparing the physical environment for the computer system. The major burden for this usually falls upon the company, but the vendor should agree to provide support, advice, and guidance.

Conversion assistance is frequently one of the concessions offered by the vendor in order to close a sale. This kind of item often is highly negotiable when competition between final vendors becomes fierce. The exact nature and scope of the conversion assistance to be provided should be spelled out in the contract.

The company may also stipulate in the contract that qualified personnel be assigned by the vendor to his project. Such a provision is generally a good idea. Vendor companies are often small. They may grow quickly and hire new personnel as a result. And it is common for new personnel to lack hands-on business experience. The company logically would wish not to provide business training for the new personnel and demand a say in the selection of personnel to be working on its project.

Another provision can specify that the company cannot be responsible for judging material written in computer jargon. For example, if a document is submitted for the company's review that contains narrative material about how a particular application will work, along with technical material such as field lengths, record layouts, blocking factors, and flowcharts, the provision can state that the company's acceptance of the material is based upon the narrative, or nontechnical, portion. This makes sense as the company should not be expected to have sufficient computer expertise to identify errors or problems in technical documents.

Attention should be given to the subject of changes during the development stages of the computer system. One might feel that changes should be prohibited altogether and the system be based on the goals and objectives set forth in the RFP. However, it frequently happens that during the writing of the detailed system specifications, a better way to accomplish something emerges. The improvement may or may not necessarily conflict with the RFP, as that document generally concerns itself with the desired end products of the system, while the detailed system specification is more concerned with the means required to accomplish those end products. It makes sense to expect change as a natural result of writing the detailed system specifications; thus, it is reasonable to provide in the contract for the possibility of change. Attention should be given to changes both in the hardware and in the software. In one instance it was agreed that changes in the hardware configuration would be considered acceptable to the vendor provided that they were made with enough lead time and involved items of hardware normally available to the vendor. Fortunately in this situation the hardware permitted a large variety of peripherals to be attached to it, and the vendor had the ability to be flexible in his purchasing arrangements. Software changes also had to be given with enough lead time to be incorporated without substantial loss in effort to the vendor. While it is difficult to predict what kinds of changes may occur and whether they will be easy or difficult to incorporate into the system's design, it is wise at least to acknowledge that change is likely and to make some effort to accommodate it.

The contract should describe the nature and quality of the documentation that the company desires its system to have. A provision that documentation may be in draft form at the time of system delivery is a reasonable and realistic one. Much change to the software will occur during its breaking-in period, generally the first three months of operation. Were the documentation required to be in final form at the time of delivery, much of it would have to be redone later, a wasted effort for everyone. Draft documentation should be sufficient for the company to judge its quality and completeness.

Performance, Maintenance, and Service Provisions

A company frequently contracts for hardware maintenance with the manufacturer of the hardware. A warranty period is usually provided during which there is no charge for maintenance. The contract can specify that if the company and the maintenance vendor are unable to draw up a contract, then the contract between the company and the software vendor will terminate if the situation so merits. The contract should acknowledge that software, too, needs maintenance and may describe the activities that should constitute software maintenance. In general, the contract should require that the vendor present solutions to problems as they are reported and provide telephone assistance during working hours. The vendor should keep up-to-date copies of the company's software and provide the manuals and documents needed by the company for its operations. In one instance, the vendor agreed as part of his software warranty to provide the first year of software maintenance at no charge and subsequent years at a reasonable charge (for at least seven years). Such provisions help protect the company's investment in software.

The vendor should be obliged to keep a maintenance log of software problems and the steps taken to correct them. This is common procedure for hardware and other industrial machinery and is also good practice for software. The company is well advised to keep such a log for itself, too. Written accounts of jobs run and problems encountered can be of immeasurable value when mysterious occurrences need to be analyzed in the future.

An important provision to include is one giving the company the right to modify its programs itself or hire outside parties to do so. This frees the company from total dependence upon a single software vendor for the life of the system. In one arrangement that was acceptable to both parties suggested software changes were to be submitted in writing to the software vendor, who would have fifteen days to approve or object to the changes. Normally, objections would be based on a judgment of harm or damage that the change might cause to the system. In the absence of any response from the vendor, approval was assumed. The vendor was compensated for the time and effort expended in reviewing the changes. Some arrangement should be worked out so that the vendor's efforts to produce a working system are protected while the company has freedom from total dependence on one vendor for the life of the system.

Representations, Warranties, and Undertakings

The vendor should warrant his system to be "merchantable" or "worthy of sale." The various attachments to the contract are declared to be the vendor's representations and warranties to that effect.

Additional assistance may be promised by the vendor. In one instance, the vendor agreed to permit the company to upgrade to newer models of the computer system at the same discount as the initially purchased equipment within a specified period. The vendor also agreed to use his best efforts to have the additional equipment put on the maintenance contract.

The vendor may also agree both to be available for future programming for a given period of time and to try to make the same people available for such projects as participated in the development of the original system. This is a realistic provision as many (if not most) companies wish to make improvements in and additions to their systems upon completion of the original development phase. It is most advantageous to have the same personnel available to make such changes.

Additional provisions can require the vendor to perform all of his services for the company primarily with full-time help (to avoid involvement with moonlighters) and to do so with minimal disruption of the company's operations.

The vendor will normally warrant that the system is capable of having standard peripheral devices connected to it and should agree to be available for evaluation and assistance in attaching nonstandard devices should they be desired. The vendor should be reasonably compensated for these efforts.

The vendor should also agree to provide training for the users of the system. Training may be included within the vendor's warranty period and available thereafter for a specified charge.

The contract should stipulate that the vendor agrees that the company gets full title to all that it is purchasing. Additional provisions can be set forth to protect the company's market position, basically by prohibiting the vendor from lessening any competitive advantage brought about by the system through providing the same advantage to direct competitors of the company. Tied into this provision is specific language about the company's right to full ownership of the software and the vendor's right to use portions of it in other systems, all of which should have been arranged to the satisfaction of both parties.

General Provisions

There should be provisions describing proprietary information and the precautions that the parties should take in order to protect it. Miscellaneous standard provisions would be present dealing with business termination considerations, expenses, insurance, notification of delays and other complicating conditions, and submission of disputes to binding arbitration. Related parties such as consultants and accountants are granted rights and powers, such as the rights to exchange proprietary information and to use licensed software in performing their tasks for their client.

Many of the provisions mentioned in this chapter will not exist in the standard contract your vendor may present to you to sign. Bear in mind that *all items are negotiable.* Rarely does a company sign a vendor's contract without making changes. It is expected that you will make some requests over and above the vendor's contract, and many if not most changes will be acceptable if you are dealing with a competent and honorable vendor.

CHAPTER FIFTEEN

A Horror Story

This chapter will not be pleasant to read. You cannot say you were not warned. Harking back to the dire predictions in Chapter 8 of things that could go wrong, most of them *do* go wrong in this story. And it is a true story, although the names of the participants are not mentioned, to protect the guilty.

They say that hindsight is twenty-twenty. At the end of the story we will discuss some reasons why the events happened as they did.

The company involved published textbooks. It had been using a service bureau that also warehoused its books to fill orders and bill customers. The service bureau–warehouse was inflexible in its operations and expensive to use. It was proposing a large price increase for the next annual contract, so the publisher decided to look for an appropriate minicomputer to perform the functions of order entry, inventory control, sales analysis, and accounts receivables on an in-house basis.

The publisher hired a consultant to assist with writing the RFP, vendor selection, and implementation. The RFP was lengthy and contained a number of ambitious plans for improving the company's existing procedures, which had been limited by the relatively inflexible operation of the service bureau.

In April the RFP was sent to six vendors. Responses were returned in May. Visits were made to the vendors' sites, and calls and visits were made to various customers of the vendors.

An extensive grid was made up, comparing the vendors on a point-by-point basis. One vendor seemed to be head and shoulders above the rest. The vendor was distributor for a middle-tier minicomputer manufacturer with a well-regarded data base management-report generator. The hardware was high quality and competitively priced. The software portion of the proposal offered a lifetime warranty, inclusion of every item of the RFP, and a price quite similar to the software prices being quoted by the other five vendors. The vendor's customer base, although small, included customers who were wildly enthusiastic about their vendor's abilities and services to them. The vendor's sales and programming staffs were investigated and had impressive records.

A decision to go with this vendor was made at the end of June. Contracts were drawn up and signed in July, and work began on the project in August.

During August, the analyst assigned by the vendor, the company's administrative manager, and the consultant began to prepare the detailed system specifications. The analyst had a quick mind and a great deal of creativity, and a number of sophisticated solutions were drawn up for the issues addressed in the RFP.

While this effort was progressing, the vendor became quite popular, as interest in minicomputer systems had begun to rise sharply. A large number of new systems were contracted for. The vendor moved to extremely posh new quarters. The size of the vendor's staff grew dramatically with the bulk of the hiring occurring at the programming staff level. Existing management resources were strained. Sales continued to grow sharply.

The specifications were completed in November. They filled a notebook four inches thick. Although the specs were both ambitious and complicated, the analyst had no concern over the vendor's ability to implement them.

Programming began at the vendor's site, with a team of three programmers led by the analyst. At the company, the consultant and manager's staff began to prepare master file information from available sources. The service bureau files had not undergone purging of any sort during their existence, so substantial effort was spent in trying to identify active customers and in repairing and correcting name and address errors. Fields such as tax codes, salesman numbers, and types of customer were added to the records being prepared for conversion to the new system. The customer file contained some eight thousand customers, many of whom were wholesalers carrying the ship-to addresses of their retail customers.

The inventory file also needed attention. It consisted of some four thousand book titles. This file went through a similar purge and cleanup process, and some fields were added, such as the book's weight and the profit center to which its sales should be posted. A large effort went into preparing the titles for printing in the annual catalogue, a task that had not been envisoned in either the RFP or the specifications.

Programming continued in December and January, although the precise status of the progress being made was not known. (It later turned out that two of the three programmers were terminated and that substantial portions of the work that had been done had to be redone.) In February a major delivery deadline was missed, but the analyst was unconcerned, saying that the delay would shortly be made up. Some program testing was done in February but was unsuccessful in that several major bugs blocked inspection of the rest of the work. The vendor's analyst continued to be optimistic.

In early March, a major decision point was faced by the company. The service bureau contract would expire at the end of April. Renewing the contract required paying a whopping price increase and committing to operations there for another year. Leaving the facility required moving all of the inventory (some 300,000 volumes) to another warehouse and using the in-house system alone starting in early May. The decision to renew or terminate had to be made immediately.

All involved felt that there was insufficient information about the status and prospects of the programming. The analyst was consulted and assured the publisher that the system would be ready for live use some eight weeks hence. In a spirit of enthusiasm, management and the consultant accepted the challenge of finishing the system in time for May operations. Thus, the decision was made to move the books and commit to the new system.

March and April had the programmers working feverishly to complete the programs. The consultant and manager were attempting to test the programs and to prepare training materials for the staff. Customer and inventory records were being converted to the new system. The conversion began to conflict with programming resources. Time began to look shorter and shorter. Major bugs were being discovered. The repair of one bug would cause three more. Hopes for a parallel run period began to fade. Testing programs was turning up more difficulties than had been imagined, and the repair of these difficulties was conflicting with the development of the remaining programs. The preprinted invoice forms arrived very late from the printer and contained a grievous error: the packing slip failed to obscure the wholesale prices of the books, making this information visible to retail customers. The enthusiasm and confidence of early March had begun to fade.

In order for a successful conversion to take place, several aspects of the new system had to be working. First, order entry functions had to be able to accept orders, set up back orders if necessary, and prepare invoices and packing slips. This required that the customer and inventory files be ready for use, as well as the order entry and invoicing programs. Second, since the company often experienced long lead times in obtaining stock, the back order mechanism had to be functioning and permit back orders to be established and released correctly. Third, the accounts receivable system had to be able to accept invoice transactions after shipments were made, accept cash receipts against them, and produce customer statements, the aged trial balance, and delinquency reports at the end of each month. This meant that the existing receivables had to have been converted from the service bureau.

The process of moving 300,000 books and keeping control of the quantities moved turned out to be more difficult than had been planned. Because of the way inventory had been stored, the same title was moved in numerous lots, requiring several transactions to record the total quantity transferred. The move was not completed until the end of May. It was decided to put all orders on back order until the move was complete rather than attempt to pick from constantly changing stock levels. This decision placed an enormous burden upon the back order handling portion of the system, which turned out to have been assigned to the most immature member of the programming team. This part of the system had been a weak link from the beginning and subsequently was redone three times.

In late May the publisher tried a back order release and invoice run. The results were disastrous. The invoices had to be destroyed, so wrong were many of them.

The conversion of the existing receivables began to encounter mysterious difficulties, as numerous old invoices were entered into the system for one customer and somehow appeared later on another customer's account. Much consternation and confusion resulted from this mixup until the cause (a subtle bug) was discovered; much work had to be redone.

System difficulties and management problems led order entry personnel to take three times longer than had been predicted to enter an order. Morale hit an all-time low. Normally three or four hundred orders were received each day by mail or telephone. The backlog of unprocessed orders began to grow rapidly, soon approached three weeks' work, and eventually amounted to double that. Certain order entry functions, such as entry of prepaid and credit card orders, did not work successfully, and such orders were delayed even further.

The second invoicing attempt was made in early June. It involved some twenty-five hundred invoices, a large percentage of which still contained major errors. The invoice register had problems, too, as its totals indicated that $30 million had been invoiced, a figure many times greater than a year's sales! Control began to be lost as overtime crews attempted to repair the errors with typewriters and to insert amended data into the system so that the proper receivables would be reflected. Production snafus exacerbated these other problems, and each invoice run had to be made twice in order to compensate for the faulty packing slip. Customer statements could not be sent because the receivables conversion was still incomplete. With the failure to invoice correctly and the backlog in entering orders, shipments were now two months behind. Customer complaints rose to an all-time high.

A third try at invoicing was made over the July 4 weekend, which was no holiday for the large number of people who worked day and night. This run was better but could not be considered successful. Now tempers flared. Meetings were held between the presidents of the two companies, and the air was thick with complaints and recriminations.

The administrative manager of the publishing company took up almost permanent quarters at a hotel across the street from the computer site. Consultant and staff members frequently spent the night in the computer room. Disk files began to fill up and space became scarce as purge routines had not been completed and several months' data had been stored without relief to the system.

Meetings continued between the parties, and the litany of horrors grew. By this point, the publisher was experiencing severe cash shortages because the inability to invoice, coupled with the inability to collect receivables, drastically reduced its income and increased its expenses.

The vendor's president attempted to make restitution by providing additional hardware at a deep discount and by assigning ten programmers to the project. The additional storage space and terminals helped, but the crash effort by the programming team did not. Indeed, the ten programmers all had to learn about the workings of the system up to that point, and senior members of the team were sidetracked by the necessity of assisting them. The analyst could not manage so large a team and began to appear harassed and haggard.

Careless and naive programming errors had plagued the system since its inception but began to have even more disastrous consequences once pressure to perform became severe. The system went down and was completely prevented from functioning on a number of occasions as operators entered responses that had not been anticipated by the programmers. (One memorable mistake occurred when an operator attempting to enter the number 1 struck the L key, a very human error. The entire system was brought to a halt.) Sensitive tasks were accessible to all operators, rather than protected by passwords, and careless menu choices more than once initiated the wrong function, often with irrecoverable results.

By fall invoicing could proceed on a regular, dependable, efficient basis. It was then discovered that during the hectic days of the summer several thousand orders had been processed by faulty programs and had been left in an indeterminate status; that is, it could not be determined whether shipments had taken place, whether back orders had been filled, whether invoices had been prepared, and whether prepayments had been posted. The publisher decided to isolate these "sick" transactions and prepare a computer letter asking the customers involved for clarification. This process took substantial time and effort but was a necessary cleanup job.

By mid-winter the accounts receivable files and programs had been repaired, cash was being posted, and customer statements could be sent out. Efforts to collect overdue accounts could resume, although they were hampered by discrepancies and customer complaints.

During the following spring invoicing could be accomplished on a regular basis with dependable results, and some semblance of order was restored to the physical inventory levels, which had been totally out of control for much of the previous period. In the summer, effort was spent reconstructing sales data. Fortunately the system had tape capabilities, and much of the data from the traumatic periods had been saved on magnetic tape and could be reanalyzed after the fact.

By this point, the relationship with the computer vendor had deteriorated dreadfully. Corrections to problems were being submitted without testing, thereby causing worse problems. Recriminations were hurled back and forth. Communication was poor at best. And the publisher was not the only customer of the vendor to be unhappy.

The consultant, who had been doing most of the repair work involving data and reconstruction, was commissioned to repair the remaining programs and to finish the incomplete portions of the system. These portions consisted of purge procedures for all areas of the system, inventory control routines, programs for taking physical inventory, and fulfillment routines for special orders. Documentation also needed preparation.

The entire system was complete more than two and a half years after the fateful day when the publisher decided to computerize. Eventually the functions ran smoothly and dependably, the backlog was gone, and some of the features of the system began to be appreciated. By this time, the vendor had exhausted his financial resources, and the vendor's company was acquired by a major creditor. The new management is still receiving complaints from customers who feel that they were poorly treated by the vendor. (It is incredible, but the former president of the vendor company has founded yet another company representing the products of another manufacturer. The industry's emphasis on sales rather than performance makes this possible. Indeed, the president has filed suit against the creditor, claiming he was forced out of business.)

So the system did get finished but at enormous cost to everyone involved. The publisher suffered losses during the period in which processing was limited and encountered much larger software development costs than were anticipated. The vendor lost money on the job, as well as a great deal of good will. The consultant spent day and night at the client site for many months and ignored almost every other professional and personal commitment. The manager lost credibility with his employer and was let go.

Why did this situation happen? What could have been done to avoid it?

The first question must be addressed to the price of the sytem. Did the vendor charge too little for too ambitious a system? Might not any vendor, caught in the position of having a loss on a fixed price system, have come up short? This is possible. At the time the proposals were being evaluated, the question of basic price levels was indeed raised. Suspicions that the job might be underpriced were allayed by the fact that other vendors had all quoted similar prices for the same RFP's contents. Could they all have underpriced the job? With the hindsight of several years, the answer is probably yes. The period in question was one of intense competition among vendors to get business, and there was also a sense of optimism about the ability to complete such work successfully. Probably the whole marketplace was caught up in a group of unreasonable expectations about the profit potential of the turnkey systems business. Certainly subsequent financial events seem to have proved that the industry was immature and needed a good shaking out, which it has gotten and probably will continue to get.

Someone once said, "There is no such thing as a free lunch." Accordingly, the vendor who undercharges has to recoup his losses somehow or else go out of business whether or not other vendors are also underpricing. So it is important to avoid buying a computer system at a loss-leader price. Rather than doom your system to failure, make the relationship with your vendor good enough so that some sort of equitable rearrangement can be made.

The system in the horror story just didn't get priced high enough. Furthermore, the specifications were too ambitious for the amount of time available. This can be a very difficult situation to avoid or correct. No one wants to volunteer his area of processing for the place where the system should be less sophisticated and helpful. The consultant may be the only party with any chance of pointing out that the plans are too grandiose to match the timetable, and even then the action may be politically unpopular, depending upon the position taken by management. Too often the proponents of a computer system within a company would rather be boiled in oil than admit that their computer plans have real limitations. Certainly in this circumstance, no one was able to convince the rest that the emperor had no clothes on.

In retrospect, the decision to plunge ahead with implementation was ill-conceived. It was based on incomplete (and in some cases totally erroneous) information, as the programming done up to that point certainly was a lot poorer than anyone realized. The decision left the publisher with no fallback; it was an all-or-nothing gamble. The risks were greater than the rewards, placing the company in a highly vulnerable position. In particular, the failure to meet the February delivery deadline was a clear signal that should have been given more attention. The difficulty of coping with severe system problems was also grossly underestimated.

The vendor contributed to the horror story by permitting his company to grow too fast. He could not manage the increased volume of commitments without compromising quality, which is exactly what happened. Instead of hiring seasoned data processing professionals to carry the increased load, he turned to inexperienced personnel. To compound the error, he failed to provide adequate training after they were hired, expecting them to learn by doing. This was indeed unfortunate for those companies on whose systems they practiced. He failed to provide necessary management as well. None of the people who starred in this horror story were stupid. Instead, they were naive and poorly managed.

No one deliberately caused the horror story. Every action by every individual involved seemed like the right thing to do at the time. There is no one act that can be singled out as the reason why. The best we can do, in reviewing the events, is to identify the major errors of judgment. I hope this horror story will make you less likely to experience one.

CHAPTER SIXTEEN

Conversion, Testing, and Preparation

Conversion of data from its existing mode into the new system is a normal concern at the time of system implementation. Testing new programs is obviously a good idea. Preparation must also precede the arrival of a new computer system. These three activities are important. While their precise nature will vary from one system to the next, there are general guidelines on how these functions should be performed.

Conversion of Data Always Occurs

Every system must have a conversion phase even if the company involved never before used any sort of computer. This is because every company has data, whether it is manually prepared or automated. Every company keeps records about customers, products, sales, purchases, and so on.

When we say data is "converted," what do we mean? Can the company's information be put into the new system exactly the way it has been found? Generally not. Whether the data has been kept in another computer or organized manually, it is the rule rather than the exception that the data goes through a cleanup and/or reformatting step before it can go into the new computer.

Conversion Is a Chance to Clean House

The natural tendency of any data file is to get out-of-date. Almost any customer file, for example, will have some useless entries in it.

Customers may have died, moved, or gone out of business, or there may be an error in the way customer information has been recorded that renders it less than totally useful. Such entries are often called "nixies" by people who work with mailing lists, meaning that these parties cannot be reached by mail. Nixies are cleaned up by sending out a mailing piece with a return address requested in order to get the invalid addresses returned by the post office. Cleaning up nixies will reduce the postal costs of subsequent mailings and solicitations; it usually is a cost-effective process. (Other kinds of files usually benefit from such cleanup processes as well.)

File Contents Are Often Expanded

In the switch to interactive minicomputer processing, streamlining an operation frequently leads to certain facts' being added to the files. Accumulating more data in the various files makes it possible for more functions to be processed by the system and renders the system more cost-effective. A common example of this is codes added to indicate whether customers are taxable and, if so, in which jurisdiction. Once customers are coded for tax calculations, tax figuring and reporting can easily be automated. This involves the addition of a tax code field to the customer record. Conversion is a logical time to look up each customer's tax code before he becomes part of the new system. These kinds of additions to files are normal features of the conversion process.

Converting Master Files and Transaction Files

The conversion of master files (permanent records that the system needs to process transactions) such as the inventory and customer master files can generally be worked on over an extended period of time and gradually completed so long as changes that occur during the conversion period are eventually included. The conversion of transaction files (for example, the accounts receivable invoice and cash receipts items that normally appear on the customer's statement at the end of each month) usually has to be completed over a shorter time period, as the transaction files themselves are shorter lived and represent data that is valid for only a certain period of time.

Master Files As Training Opportunities in a Manual Conversion

Since the conversion of master files can generally be done under conditions of less pressure, this kind of conversion is an excellent opportunity for operator training. The data involved is usually familiar and nonthreatening to the company's personnel. An operator keying customer names and addresses and other associated data into a well-written program will become totally at ease with the new system within a matter of hours or days. The operator can view the results of keying on the screen and make necessary corrections or adjustments. Converting in this "manual" way is of course required if records previously were kept manually. Even when records were previously kept in a computer system, however, this kind of conversion is often done intentionally. The previous system's records are printed out on paper. Decisions are made about purging or discarding data. Corrections and additions are entered for the remaining records, which are then used as source documents in the keying process. Thus, the functions of purging, correcting, and adding new facts to the file are combined with operator training in this kind of a conversion.

A manual conversion sometimes isn't possible with a large volume of records to be converted. These files then have to be prepared on a machine-readable medium (usually magnetic tape) and read into the new system using a special, one-time conversion routine that reformats the data as required. Data that needs to be purged, corrected, or augmented is taken care of later, using the new system's file maintenance routines.

Conversion of Transaction Files

The conversion of transaction files usually has to be done with a fair amount of control, which means *balancing* to some predetermined total after entry is completed. For example, the dollar sum of a converted accounts receivable file should be the same in the new system as it was in its old mode before conversion. In reality, it would be impossible to accomplish the entire conversion and then expect to balance the two figures. They would never agree; there are too many opportunities for error.

Generally, if the transactions are being keyed manually, the job is divided into smaller batches, ideally of the size that can be keyed in a half day or less. Totals for each batch are prepared in advance with an adding machine. The operator enters the batch and signals to the program when the batch has been completed. The program then provides the total for the batch. Next, the machine derived total is compared to the adding machine total. Some mechanism, either a listing or a screen reviewing function, is provided to locate errors if the totals disagree. Corrections and/or adjustments are made. When the two totals agree, the batch is balanced and work may begin on the next batch. This kind of balancing procedure detects transactions that are skipped (it is easy to turn two documents over instead of one!), keyed in error, or keyed more than once. Once all of the batches have been keyed and balanced, the sum of the batches should equal the total of the transactions both in the old system and in the new.

When automatic conversions are performed using conversion programs reading files from some machine-readable medium, the program then provides totals of the transactions converted at the end of the job. If the conversion differs from the known totals before conversion, there is something wrong with the conversion process or program. Occasionally, it has been found that the totals produced by the old system were wrong.

Conversion Time Can Be Traumatic

Many users approach their new systems the way some people approach the New Year. They make strong resolutions to reform their ways and allow only clean data to enter the system. These intentions are commendable and very much to be desired. Most people would agree that it is not sensible to have a very sophisticated, new computer churning out the same errors that the old system produced. But this goal often places a great deal of pressure upon the operators of the new system. Operators may find themselves facing an unfamiliar system, with the clear message from management that they will be in serious trouble if so much as one clerical error is entered. These fears lower morale and motivation and should be replaced with a balanced perspective. Management should try to communicate the message that it hopes that everyone will cooperate in making the system successful and that the system will assist personnel in many ways, for instance, by protecting them from making serious errors. This approach is consistent with the system design and programming techniques discussed earlier and will make the conversion period less traumatic for everyone.

Conversion time is a difficult time in that most companies are not likely to be sufficiently staffed for this task, which has to be accomplished in addition to normal duties. Often conversion gets pushed into overtime or weekends. Even when extra or temporary staff are brought in to assist, some permanent staff member will have the extra burden of managing their efforts. Accordingly, companies frequently phase their conversion activities. As different applications are completed, the conversions necessary to implement them are accomplished in stages.

Program Testing

Testing the vendor's programs can be very complicated. Normally the programmer who writes a program is responsible for testing his own work. This isn't always a sufficient kind of testing—for several reasons. First, it is only human not to think of conditions that have not occurred to you! The programmer has made certain assumptions about the conditions to protect his program against and may not be able to recognize additional conditions he has not thought of. Simply because he brings a fresh perspective to the task, an outsider can often find difficulties in a program that has been tested extensively by its writer. In addition, as I discussed in Chapter 5, not all programmers have a mature attitude toward their work. Their immaturity generally shows itself in the quality of their testing, as they make the basic error of assuming that their programs *will* work instead of taking the realistic, mature position that they *won't* work.

Program testing is one of the tests for which you may want to engage a consultant. An experienced data processing professional will be able to do a much more thorough job of program testing than can a person with very little experience. The novice user can make some progress in testing by himself, however, if he follows a few general concepts.

Be Calm and Methodical

The tester should locate himself in a quiet place where he can work uninterruptedly with the system. Let us assume that he is seated at a terminal and has a particular application that is ready for testing. Let us also assume that he is at the vendor's site and has been assured that he will be unable to harm live data or program files in his activities. (The tester should always determine that system files and programs cannot be affected by his actions before starting. Testing applications on live systems is extremely difficult and dangerous and should not be attempted without help.)

It is important when testing to keep a careful record of the actions taken by the tester. By definition, unexpected results will occur, and it is most difficult to be in the position of wondering "Now, what did I key before that strange thing happened?" There are several ways to record what is being done. One obvious way is with a tape recorder. You can also keep careful notes as the operations take place or have a helper do so. The tester can also limit the keying to one or two simple transactions, although this lessens the realistic qualities of the testing.

Keep a Bug List

It is important to establish good records about the results of the testing. A "bug list" is essential. Bugs may be recorded in straight chronological sequence as they are discovered. Often, however, a bug list is more useful if bugs (true program errors) are separated from questions and improvements. Next to each entry ought to be a place to record its priority, or how important the correction or resolution of the item is to the success of the system. Remember that resolution of these items will generally conflict with development of other applications, so that it is essential to be able to distinguish among items that must be resolved immediately, those that can wait a while, and those that may never be worth taking care of. Space should also be left for indicating the resolution of the item when it occurs. Some bug books devote an entire page to each bug, question, or problem, so that the resolution or answer can be recorded in a fair amount of detail and used for reference and analysis.

Test Basic Program Execution and Linkage

The most primitive level of testing is to determine whether the functions really do execute as advertised on their menus. You may want to review the concept of operating the system through a series of menus, as described in Chapter 10. The tester should methodically attempt to execute each item on each menu for the application being tested, making sure that the proper function occurs in each instance. It is surprisingly easy to create a well-written program that functions correctly but fail to link it to the appropriate menu! This basic level of testing will identify such problems.

Test the Instructions to the Operator

The tester should next follow to the letter the directions given by the system or by any available "run book" or documentation. Directions should be followed exactly and the tester should judge whether they leave room for misunderstanding or confusion or are clear and concise. Ask whether the messages given by the system are helpful and specific. The tester should place himself in the position of a novice operator (i.e., convince himself that he is uncertain what to do) and make the commonsense judgment whether he is being given sufficient guidance to prevent errors and problems. This kind of testing helps avoid numerous problems later and enables training to proceed more effectively throughout the life of the system.

Test a Controlled Batch of Work

Once it has been determined that the proper functions execute when called for, and that the communications with the operator are appropriate, it needs to be determined that a representative batch of work can be handled satisfactorily by the system.

The batch of work should be prepared in advance of the testing session with a fair amount of thought. The batch should be as representative as possible of the range of transactions normally performed for the application in question. Often the clerical personnel involved with the application can be helpful in developing a list of the features to be included in the batch of work. For example, if a batch of work were being made up to test an order entry function, the following kinds of orders might be included:

—an order from a retail customer
—an order from a wholesale customer
—an order from a taxable customer

—an order for which tax should not be charged
—an order for products that are not in stock
—an order for more items than will fit on one invoice page
—an order involving a quantity discount
—an order charged to a credit card
—an order with a full prepayment
—an order with a partial prepayment
—an order with a prepayment involving a back order
—an order from a customer whose credit has been suspended
—an order that is assumed canceled before shipping

There may also be compound conditions of the above, involving several aspects at once. The list can be quite extensive, depending upon the number and types of features that the system is supposed to have. Real orders may be copied to use in the test, or orders may be invented, making them as realistic as possible. Finally, it is good to refer to the RFP to insure that none of the system's projected features has been forgotten in preparing the test batch.

The batch of orders may be entered into the system several times. During the first attempt, the functions that do not perform correctly will be identified and can be listed in the bug book for correction. Once the system handles all of the functions correctly, then the batch can be treated as an overall group of orders. Totals for the batch can be followed through the system, making sure that nothing is lost from one step to the next. For example, if a booked orders report is part of the system, all of the orders in the batch should be listed on it, and its total should agree with known (prepared) totals for the batch. The invoicing process should produce the expected totals on the invoices and invoice register, which then should be reflected in the incremental addition to accounts receivable once that posting has been completed. The remaining orders should be accounted for as back or canceled orders. Predictable totals should be tracked through the sales history, inventory control, salesperson commission, or any other applications that are recipients of the flow of order data. In this way, the prepared batch of work can assist in establishing that the system has the proper controls and overall integrity of data from one application to another.

The third area in which the batch approach is helpful is in obtaining timings for the processes being tested. The batch of work, if it is truly representative of the kinds of data that the system eventually will process under live conditions, will provide the first opportunity to determine how long the operator and system functions will actually be taking. Up until that point, timings are only estimates. With firm data about the number of minutes required to enter an order, print a hundred invoices, say, post receivables, and so forth, staff loads can be calculated and plans made for live operations that were not possible previously.

Test Terrible Transactions

A final kind of testing is to test the most difficult and complicated transactions that can be found. It is often a good idea, or at least an amusing one, to ask clerical personnel who are actively involved in the application being tested to make a collection of the nastiest transactions that pass across their desks for the several months preceding the testing. Staff members then begin to enjoy (!) seeing a dreadful transaction come along, for then they can make a copy of it for their collection and feel a part of the process of testing the new system. Frequently this approach will uncover some aspect of processing that had not been anticipated by the system's designers. Although this discovery can be unnerving, it is better to know these deficiencies at testing time than during live operations. Usually some way to process these terrible transactions can be developed. An example of a terrible transaction might be an order from a customer on credit hold that was accompanied by a partial prepayment and involved a back order!

Preparation Activities

Conversion and testing activities may involve a very limited number of prople within the company. General preparation activities are best accomplished when they involve a larger group of people.

The Team Approach

The team approach is often successful. The team ideally consists of the vendor's project leader, the consultant (if one has been utilized), and a representative from senior company management and from each of the application areas that will be part of the new system. The team should be formed well in advance of the implementation of the system; in some cases it is formed during the writing of the RFP (although the vendor's representative is not present at that stage).

The team should have frequent meetings and good communications. The monthly tasks memorandum mentioned in Chapter 14 can be used to advantage in recording progress since the last meeting and in setting out objectives and goals for the next working period.

The team should be concerned with the overall aspects of preparation, as well as with the individual areas represented by the team members. A schedule should be drawn up that meets with the satisfaction of all. It should include the implementation, testing, conversion, parallel run, and cutover times for each application.

As testing progresses, the bug lists should be discussed and reviewed at team meetings, with consideration given to the realistic assignment of priorities to the repair of bugs. After all, by definition every bug cannot be the most important and the group should be forced to work out an arrangement in which all application areas feel they are getting their fair share of the vendor's bug repair efforts.

The importance of the team approach cannot be overemphasized. It is a major factor in the success of the system, virtually insuring cooperation from all areas of company management.

Staff Training

Do expect that company personnel who have not worked with systems or terminals before will be apprehensive. This is a natural reaction to an unknown experience. A good way to reduce and quell such apprehension is to have staff members visit the vendor's site in small groups early in the implementation process. Often, a half hour playing one of the ubiquitous computer games can introduce a person to the workings of a terminal and the nature of interactive processing and provide him with a successful first impression of the way a computer works. Many of the current games are ingenious and amusing and can be very helpful in bridging that initial gap. For this reason, you might ask that the games be put on your system, too!

Staff members who are given a chance to participate in conversion and testing activities also can receive valuable training. Staff training will occur on both a direct and an indirect basis. We discussed the philosophy of good systems design in previous chapters. The amount of help that the system can give its operators can very much reduce the requirements for formal training throughout the life of the system. Interestingly, the nature of training within a company will also change once the computer helps the operator to make the right entry. Then training content becomes more concentrated around the subject of company procedures and policies, or it may emphasize peripheral areas that augment the computer system such as how to use the customer file cabinets.

Staff operators who will operate specialized equipment, such as the tape and disk drives and the printer, will receive training in those aspects of system operations from the vendor or manufacturer. Personnel who become interested or proficient in computer operations may also be sent to classes in programming, system design, or use of generalized retrieval languages. Such classes are often given by the vendor, manufacturer, or local adult education center.

Parallel Operations

This subject is quite difficult to discuss in the abstract, as the need for parallel operations varies widely from implementation to implementation. Its uses are greatly misunderstood.

Most potential computer users fail to acknowledge the difficulties inherent in trying to operate two systems at once. There is a vivid and accurate analogy in riding two horses at once, standing with one foot on each saddle. Yes, it is true that the rider has two alternatives and can decide to ride either horse and abandon the other at will. But the difficulty of maintaining those two alternatives at once is enormous! The same is true of parallel operations. Most companies simply do not have sufficient resources to operate both their old and new systems simultaneously for long periods until a decision is made to abandon one or the other.

The goal in parallel operations is to keep the maximum number of *options* open to management with the least effort, that is, to avoid vulnerability and keep a fallback position. The aim is to exercise the complete cycle of processes that make up a function in the shortest amount of time to guarantee that they all work before committing to them. For example, if an accounts receivable application is being converted, the major functions that need to work are those that occur at the month's end. Virtually each month is processed in the same way, and few if any functions occur at year-end. To operate in parallel successfully through one month-end cycle should be sufficient. Additional months of parallel processing will not provide any additional benefits and will strain the staff's resources unnecessarily. Once it has been determined that the month-end aged trial balance, customer statements, and delinquency reports are all working properly and that the daily functions such as invoice posting and cash receipts are working, parallel operations of accounts receivable should end.

Another aspect of determining whether sufficient time has been planned for parallel processing is the degree of change that the old system has gone through in evolving to the new one. When two systems that are substantially different are operated in parallel, a great deal of effort has to be spent reconciling the differences between them. Yet the fact that they were different was already known and need not have been proved! If the two ways of processing tally transactions up in very different ways or are grossly divergent in their basic assumptions, remember that an enormous amount of work will be required to crosscheck the results of the one against those of the other and the attendant benefits may not exist.

CHAPTER SEVENTEEN

The Loose Ends

The process of finishing a system is an ambiguous one. As the child who visited New York City said, "It's nice, but when are they going to finish it?" Likewise, some systems never stop being changed or improved. And it really is not surprising when you consider that most successful businesses are in a constant state of growth and change. There is really no reason to assume that the computer systems that help them operate would stay unchanged over long periods of time.

Now that we have accepted the idea that the system may become stable but won't likely be stagnant, what is the best way to cope with this reality?

Expand the Bug Book into a Bug and Project Book

As implementation progresses, the number of bugs should dwindle. In their place will probably be a large number of items in the improvement category. Some of these improvements may indeed be full-fledged projects on their own, or they may consist of entirely new applications for the system. It will be obvious that the original RFP and detailed system specifications did not include these projects.

With the experience of the initial implementation, you will find decisions concerning additional project implementations infinitely easier. The team that played an important role during the implementation of the original system either should still be functioning or can be resurrected easily. The team can consider the feasibility of potential projects and schedule their implementation if it decides to go ahead. The entire process is similar to that followed in the initial phases of the system; however, at this point many more pieces are in place and to proceed is much easier.

Make Sure Good Security Habits Have Been Established

After the initial stages of fright have passed, a period of complacency about system operations may set in. It is important that these feelings of complacency not be allowed to become permanent in the area of data security. The management personnel in charge of the system should insure that periodic file copies are made and stored correctly, that fire drills are held frequently, that passwords and menu protection features are functioning to limit unauthorized access to the system, and in general that the system's operations are secure.

Discourage Finger Pointing

Some fault can always be found with the operations of the computer system. Computers are frequently the object of finger pointing, interdivisional mud slinging, power plays, and other company political activities. It is crucial to establish and support the idea that the computer belongs to everyone. A well-orchestrated team implementation approach helps in this effort. One division should not be saddled with blame for the inactions of all the rest!

Obviously the emotional environment surrounding a computer installation is very much a function of the particular individuals involved. The individual who runs a function and is considered Public Enemy Number One by his associates will no doubt operate a computer with the same reputation. It is not easy to arrange that the computer be widely appreciated within a company. And yet it *is* worth giving some thought to ways that might work in your company. A company whose management works together and supports the computer system is much more likely to get its money's worth from the system than is the company whose computer is the focus of bitter in-fighting. Of course the quickest way for a computer to become widely accepted and appreciated is for it to work really well and to be of genuine assistance to its users. Even when that is the case, however, political games may start. Top management should be alert for such a situation and be ready to take whatever action is most appropriate to correct it.

Make Sure Documentation Gets Finished

Documentation is the most common kind of loose end after the major effort of implementation is over. Perhaps it is only human nature not to want to write about things that are seemingly finished. It is important that management dispel the notion that things are finished before the documentation is also finished. Scheduling deadlines for documentation before new projects are started is also a good idea. Most of all, extend encouragement and appreciation to those whose job it is to prepare documentation (even the vendor).

Spent Time Analyzing Results

After the major push to get your system running, find some quiet moments and review what really happened. With the benefit of hindsight decide what went wrong and why. Most people concentrate on analyzing the disastrous parts of what happened. There is nothing wrong with doing this, provided that something can thereby be learned. But often, the same situation will not present itself exactly the same way the next time. It is important, too, to analyze *what went right* and why. The aspects of the successful result can be encouraged and promoted the next time a job needs to be done.

Share Experiences with Other Users

User groups are becoming more common among users of the same manufacturer or vendor. Typically such groups hold monthly meetings at which members share food, drink, and experiences. It can be very helpful to participate in such a group. First, an informal network is forged of people who can help each other in terms of equipment and facilities. Then, users can share their experiences. This kind of give-and-take can benefit everyone involved. It is always interesting to see how another user solved a problem you may have faced. And you may pick up some ideas that are highly useful.

CHAPTER EIGHTEEN

What Are You Going to Do Now?

Having read almost all of this book, you are most likely at a point of major decision. Do you go ahead with plans for a minicomputer system or pass? In hopes of adding a little perspective to the picture, let's review some of the areas that the book has addressed.

You became more comfortable with concepts and terminology in Chapter 1. You began, I hope, to feel that you might be able to converse with computer people. In Chapter 2 you found that there really is no good definition of a minicomputer but got a better idea of what it is. Chapter 3 introduced you to the machinery and devices associated with minicomputer business systems and described the roles played by each. Some of the features that you might want to consider were described.

Chapter 4 gave you a better idea of how a computer actually operates and explored various kinds of systems and programs. The process of programming was described in Chapter 5, where the nature of the job and its frustrations were illustrated. A handy test for evaluating programmers and some advice on preparing good programs were included.

Chapter 6 enumerated the preparation and maintenance requirements of today's equipment and gave you an idea of the obligations involved in having a system. Chapter 7 reviewed the roles being played by business minicomputers today and the kinds of systems they have been replacing. It also mentioned ways in which one might identify the sorts of applications that could be computerized most cost-effectively.

The question of feasibility was explored in greater detail in

Chapter 8, which identified both right and wrong reasons for wanting a computer system. The major factors of benefits and costs were described, and some traditional myths about computerizing were debunked.

Chapter 9 gave specific guidance for writing the request for proposal. The areas to be covered were listed in detail, and a sample text was included. Chapter 10 described a number of good design features that could be incorporated in the business applications common to most companies. Advice on implementing successful applicatons such as accounts receivable and accounts payable was given.

The subject of choosing and using a computer consultant was discussed in Chapter 11. Chapter 12 explored the various kinds of hardware and software vendors that might be investigated and explained the kinds of relationships available.

Chapter 13 analyzed the process of evaluating vendor proposals in great detail, describing a grid-making process and giving specific direction on how to use it.

Chapter 14 reviewed the areas of concern in preparing a contract with the chosen vendor.

A true story was told in Chapter 15. The story was scary but useful in providing a better understanding of things that can go wrong and how to prevent them.

Conversion, testing, and preparation activities were discussed in Chapter 16, which described how to test programs, record problems, and convert data to the new system. Chapter 17 examined various loose ends and mentioned several nontechnical procedures to be followed in making your computer system work.

This book has tried to cover the entire process of adopting a computer system. You should know by now whether you want to proceed with such a system. The benefits of computerizing have been described. So have the liabilities, costs, risks, dangers, and problems. An objective judge might declare that the darker side of the process has had more emphasis than the lighter one in this book. This probably means that if you still want to go ahead, you are likely to be making the correct decision. But after all, they pay chief executives to make hard decisions. Good luck!

Glossary

Alphabetic Field	A field that normally contains only letters, such as the name of a city.
Alphameric Field	A field that contains both numbers and letters, such as a street address.
Analyst	A person who determines the overall functions to be performed by a computer system and blocks out the major tasks the system will do.
APL	A popular programming language; the name stands for "a programming language."
Applications Software	The programs and procedures that perform the specific applications a system runs, such as accounts receivable.
Applications Programmers	Programmers who write the programs that perform the user's applications, such as accounts payable.
Audible Tones	Beeps or clicks that can be sounded by a cathode ray terminal under program control.
BASIC	A programming language in wide use on minicomputers; the name stands for "beginners all-purpose symbolic instruction code."
Batch Mode	A mode of operating only one job at a time on a computer; the data nec-

essary for that one job exists in the computer only during that job.

Baud Rate The speed at which devices exchange information over communications lines, generally expressed in bits per second.

Benchmarking A traditional technique for evaluating different computer systems by running the same job on each and comparing the time required for completion.

Bit A shortened form of binary digit. Combinations of bits identify the various numbers and letters in data. Eight bits make up one byte.

Bug A fault or error in a computer program.

Byte One character of data, such as a letter or a digit.

Cathode Ray Tube A computer terminal combining a televisionlike display screen with a keyboard.

Central Processing Unit The part of a computer that contains its memory and logic circuits and controls the entire system.

Channel See Track.

Character Printer A printer that prints one character after another.

COBOL A popular programming language; the name stands for "common business oriented language."

Compiler A special program that converts programming language into machine language.

Computer Program A collection of instructions that together perform a particular function.

CPU See Central Processing Unit.

CRT See Cathode Ray Tube.

Cursor A flashing character on a cathode ray tube that is positioned at a desired field to indicate where keying should next take place.

Custom Programs Programs specifically tailored, or customized, for a particular user.

Data The information that a system contains about its customers, receivables, etc.; the facts and figures processed by the system.

Debugging The process of identifying and removing errors from computer programs.

Density A term used to describe the distance between the magnetized spots on magnetic tape; the higher the density, the more data can be transcribed on a given length of tape.

Devices Terminals, printers, or other equipment used in the exchange of information between computer and user.

Disk Drives Equipment that physically contains and rotates the disks and moves the heads that read, and write upon, them.

Diskette A small, flexible disk pack with limited capacity but extremely portable and economical.

Disk Pack The actual recording surface of a disk, usually including a protective cover.

Distributor The representative of a manufacturer in a particular area.

Dual Intensity A feature on some cathode ray tubes allowing for characters to be displayed, under program control, in either a brighter or a dimmer intensity.

Edit Procedure A procedure that tests the validity of data; a listing of errors detected is usually produced.

Field A discrete piece of information within a particular record.

File	A collection of information manifesting a common relationship; a group of records.
Floppy Disk	See Diskette.
Flowchart	A technique for describing and documenting the individual steps within a process.
FORTRAN	A popular programming language developed for scientific and industrial uses; the name stands for "formula translation."
Hardware	The physical equipment and devices of the computer system.
Inches per Second	The speed at which a magnetic tape drive can advance the tape in the drive.
Input-Output Device	A device that can both take and receive information.
Interactive Processing	A mode of processing in which the computer is updated almost instantaneously; there is generally some form of give-and-take dialogue between the system and its operators.
IPS	See Inches per Second.
K	Roughly a thousand (actually 1,024) characters of data.
Keypunch Machine	A keyboard driven machine that punches characters into cardboard cards.
Language	See Machine Language and Programming Language.
Line Printer	A printer that prints an entire line at one time.
Machine Language	The language that each machine understands.
Magnetic Tape	A sequential recording device used to exchange data with computer systems; resembles audio tape used in tape recorders.
Mainframe Computers	A name given to a class of computers,

	generally large, centralized, and operated in batch mode.
Memory	The part of the central processing unit that contains the instructions and data actively being processed.
Menu	A technique to display a list of alternatives to an operator and request a choice of one of them.
Modem	A specialized device used to attach a computer or one of its devices to a communications line.
Numeric Field	A field that normally contains only numbers, such as a dollar amount or a domestic zip code.
OEM	See Original Equipment Manufacturer.
Operating System	A common term for a collection of system software that makes a particular system operate.
Original Equipment Manufacturer	A company that assembles computer systems from components made by different hardware manufacturers.
Packaged Programs	Programs created for the general needs of a number of users.
Paper Tape	A sequential access method of recording data by punching holes in paper tape.
Partition	A segment of memory allocated to a particular use.
Partitioning	A technique of fixed allocations of memory for particular uses.
Password	A technique for limiting access to sensitive programs and data to authorized persons by requesting entry of a secret word.
Printed Circuit Boards	Boards containing electronic components that operate the computer itself and can be replaced modularly by the serviceperson.
Programming Language	A language developed for people to

give instructions to computers more easily.

Programming Specifications A document detailing the precise programming steps that must be taken to create a given application.

Programming Template A plastic device that assists a programmer in tracing the symbols used in flowcharting.

Programs The instructions the system follows in order to process its data.

Punched Cards Cardboard cards containing punches made by keypunch machines and used to exchange data with a computer system.

Random Access Device A device that can access data in a random fashion, or in a sequence other than that in which it was recorded.

Real-time Processing A mode of processing data such that the computer is updated almost instantaneously rather than after the next batch of work is processed.

Record A member of a file.

Request for Proposal A document written by a potential user requesting bids on his requirements for a computer system.

Response Time The time required for a system to respond to a user's request.

Reverse Image A feature on some cathode ray tubes allowing for some characters to be displayed, under program control, with the opposite background from that of other characters.

RFP See Request for Proposal.

RPG A popular programming language, especially on IBM systems; the name stands for "report program generator."

Screen See Cathode Ray Tube.

Sequential Access Device A device that records and accesses

	data in a fixed sequence, as a tape recorder would do.
Serial Printer	A printer that prints one character after another.
Software	The programs and procedures that make the system run on the hardware.
Software House	A company that sells computer programming services or packages.
Storage	The part of the computer that contains instructions and data for jobs not actively being processed.
System Software	The programs and procedures that instruct the system how to operate its own devices.
Systems Programmers	A specialized group of programmers who work for computer manufacturers and create the systems that operate the equipment for the user.
Terminal	A general term for a cathode ray tube or other input-output device that communicates with the operator.
Track	A term used to describe the scheme for encoding data on magnetic tape; seven or nine tracks are common.
Turnkey	A marketing strategy of selling computer systems with hardware and software combined into one package. The customer is theoretically to "turn the key" and begin using his finished system.
VDT	See Cathode Ray Tube.
Video Display Terminal	See Cathode Ray Tube.

Bibliography

General Computer Management

Computer Handbook for Senior Management, by Douglas B. Hoyt. New York: Macmillan, 1978. A good introduction to a variety of subjects of interest to those responsible for computer management who lack a technical computer background.

Technical Assistance in Preparing Computer Contracts

Data Processing Contracts, by Dick H. Brandon and Sidney Segelstein. New York: Van Nostrand Reinhold, 1976. The definitive reference on computer contracts.

Periodicals on Computer Developments and Vendor Offerings

Computer Business News. A weekly newspaper published by Computer Business News, 375 Cochituate Road, Framingham MA 01701. $15/year. Articles emphasize the business and financial aspects of developments in the computer industry.

Computer Career News. A biweekly newspaper published by Computer Career News, 708 Third Avenue, New York NY 10017. Controlled circulation or $25/year. Articles emphasize the personnel aspects of data processing.

Computer Decisions. A monthly magazine published by Hayden Publishing, 50 Essex Street, Rochelle Park NJ 07662. Controlled circulation. Timely feature articles on subjects in the field of computer system management. Reviews of new products.

Computerworld. A weekly newspaper published by CW Communications, 375 Cochituate Road, Framingham MA 01701. $30/year. Includes a variety of feature articles and reports on all aspects of the computer industry, including both large and small computer systems, hardware, software, minicomputers, communications. Widely read in the computer industry.

Creative Computing. A monthly magazine published by Creative Computing, P.O. Box 789-M, Morristown NJ 07960. $15/year. Articles and features directed toward the home or hobby computer user. Reviews of new equipment. Listings of computer games and programs.

Datamation. A monthly magazine published by Technical Publishing, 1301 South Grove Avenue, Barrington IL 60010. Controlled circulation or $36/year. Articles and features on overall aspects of data processing and large systems. Good for identifying trends and areas of concern to the entire data processing field.

ICP Interface Small Business Management. A quarterly magazine published by International Computer Programs, 9000 Keystone Crossing, Indianapolis IN 66240. Controlled circulation or $10/year. Specializes in articles on computer topics for small businesses. Lists software resources for small systems. Good resource for locating software packages for minicomputers.

Information Systems News. A monthly newspaper published by CMP Publications, 333 East Shore Road, Manhasset NY 11030. Controlled circulation or $17.50/year. Feature articles about all aspects of information systems.

Interactive Computing. A bimonthly magazine published by and for members of the Association of Computer Users, P.O. Box 9003, Boulder CO 80301. Membership $25/year. Membership benefits include a newsletter and *Benchmark Reports*, comparing manufacturers' offerings of small computer systems.

Mini-Micro Systems. A monthly magazine published by Cahners Publishing, 221 Columbus Avenue, Boston MA 02116. Controlled circulation or $30/year. Good feature articles on hardware and software trends for small systems and specific manufacturers' offerings. Book reviews.

Office Products News. A monthly newspaper published by United Technical Publications, 645 Stewart Avenue, Garden City NY 11530. Controlled circulation. Articles and feature reports concentrating on word processing and small office and business systems.

Small Business Computers. A bimonthly magazine published by SBC Publishing, 33 Watchung Plaza, Montclair NJ 07042. Controlled circulation or $12/year. Practical information on sources for hardware and software for small computer systems. Articles on appropriate uses for each.

Reference Materials

Datapro Research Corporation, Moorestown Road, Delran NJ 08075. Publishes a number of reference services updated on a subscription basis.

Each is authoritative, nonbiased, well written, and easy to use. The basic service, **Datapro 70,** provides a wealth of information about all sorts of computers, vendors, peripherals, and areas of interest ($650 for a new subscription). **Datapro Reports on Minicomputers** ($550) is a similarly useful resource. Other Datapro services include banking automation, retail automation, data communications, software, word processing, copiers and duplicators, telecommunications, and the automated office.

Used Computer Equipment Resources

Computer Hotline. Box 1373, Fort Dodge IA 50501. Controlled circulation. Lists a wide variety of computer hardware that users want to buy and sell.

Minicomputer Supplies Resources

Quill Minicomputer and Word Processing Supplies Catalog. 3200 Arnold Lane, Northbrook IL 60062.

Fidelity Products Catalog. 705 Pennsylvania Avenue South, Minneapolis MN 55425.

Index

O

P

R